THE LIFE AND WORK OF BRANWELL BRONTË

JAMES T KELLY

CONTENTS

PART III

AND THE WEARY ARE AT REST BY BRANWELL BRONTË

PART IV

THE LETTERS OF BRANWELL BRONTË

ABOUT THE AUTHOR

James began working on this book while studying English Literature at the University of East Anglia, where he wrote his dissertation on the poetry of Branwell Brontë. Since then he has been distracted by a career as a professional writer, working as a copywriter as well as a novelist. He's pleased he's finally written this book, and he hopes you enjoy it.

jamestkelly.com

twitter.com/branwellbronte

ISBN 978-1-910599-27-3

Skerry Books Ltd

To my sister, who insists on calling him "Bramwell Brown"

INTRODUCTION

"What are you working on?"

"A book about Branwell Brontë."

"Bramwell who?"

That's how most conversations about this book started. I would go on to explain that the Brontë sisters (of *Jane Eyre*/*Wuthering Heights*/*Agnes Grey* fame) had a brother. I would tell them that he was a writer too, even a published poet, but that not many people knew that.

Some people knew who Branwell was. "Oh, the Brontë brother. He was an alcoholic, wasn't he? And a drug addict? And he died standing up?" And I would tell them a bit, in the end, and no, in that order. And that he was a writer too, even a published poet, but that not many people knew that.

And some people knew that Branwell was a writer too. "But he wasn't very good, was he?" And I would tell them yes, he was actually. He was published, before his sisters in fact, but that not many people knew that.

There's a bit of a theme emerging, isn't there?

Branwell's story isn't well known and, if someone is aware of Branwell, they've usually been fed what I think of as the Branwell Myth:

that he was nothing more than a talentless drunk and an addict. Branwell didn't do himself any favours; he *was* a drunk and an addict in the last years of his life. But many writers have tarred his entire life with the brush of a few years. And why?

First Elizabeth Gaskell wrote an apologist biography of Charlote Brontë, attempting to explain the supposed crudity of Charlotte's work by blaming others, such as Branwell, for bringing crudity into her life. Gaskell downplayed Charlotte's flaws and magnified everyone else's, and Branwell suffered as a result. Well-meaning friends looking to salvage their friends reputation then claimed that Branwell was the true author of *Wuthering Heights*.

The backlash took Gaskell's biography and added decades of scorn and dismissal. The popular narrative is that Branwell was a talentless wreck, and I might have believed it if my university hadn't had a copy of Tom Winnifrith's *Poems of Branwell Brontë*.

Branwell could write. And he wrote well.

I decided to write about Branwell in my dissertation, and my professors told me my work would be a good foundation for a research doctorate. But literary criticism has a small audience, and I'm a storyteller at heart. I wanted to tell the story of Branwell's life to everyone, and thereby rehabilitate him back into the Brontë story.

That's what this book is all about: an effort to make it easy for anyone, be they student or idly curious, to find out more about Branwell. I've made an effort to be impartial when I tell his story; there's no point in trying to make him out to be a saint. And I've done my best to make a clear distinction between fact and my own opinion, specifically the chapters about Alexander Percy and *Wuthering Heights*. I think these chapters answer questions about Branwell's supposed affair with a married women and his authorship of *Wuthering Heights*, but they are opinions I have arrived at based on the facts available; they are not facts themselves.

It's up to you to decide if you agree with my opinions. And if you disagree, that's okay. Great, in fact. This book isn't meant to be the authoritative volume on Branwell, the final answer and full stop. It's meant to be more of a beginning. A reboot, if you will. An attempt to reset the conversation, to start it again with the facts and a better perspective, or a jumping-on point for newcomers to the discussion.

To that end, I've tried to cover what I feel are the big Branwell issues. I've included the story of Branwell's life, answering key questions regarding the affair he supposedly had with a married woman, whether he had an illegitimate child, and whether he was the true author of *Wuthering Heights*.

But I also believe Branwell deserves to be remembered for his work, so I've also taken a look at that work, and reproduced it so you can judge for yourself. You'll find all of his published poetry alongside a few examples of his unpublished work, at the back of this book.

This book is for anyone who wants to read Branwell's work, for anyone who wants to know if he was really as bad as everyone says, for anyone who wants to know the true story of the forgotten Brontë. And for anyone who ever said, "Bramwell who?"

PART I

THE LIFE OF BRANWELL BRONTË

THE LIFE OF BRANWELL BRONTË

BRANWELL DIED FROM TUBERCULOSIS AT THE AGE OF 31. WEAKENED BY months of drink and drugs in an effort to numb the devastation of a lost love, he died in his father's bed, where he had slept since he accidentally set fire to his own bed sheets. And what did his older sister, Charlotte, have to say upon his tragic, untimely demise?

> I do not weep from a sense of bereavement – there is no prop withdrawn, no consolation torn away, no dear companion lost – but for the wreck of talent, the ruin of promise, the untimely dreary extinction of what might have been a burning and a shining light.[1]

Harsh words in the wake of her brother's death, but no less harsh than her description of his illness. She told her publisher how Branwell had 'led us a sad life with his absurd and often intolerable conduct'[2] even as she acknowledged he had 'two or three times fallen down in fits'[3]. Charlotte's conduct could be seen as cruel or unloving, but the truth of it is she was only bitterly disappointed.

Great Expectations

Patrick Branwell Brontë, known as Branwell, was the fourth child of six, and the only boy. Born 26th June 1817, he inherited a name from each parent: Patrick from his father, Patrick Brontë, and Branwell from his mother, Maria Branwell. Branwell's eldest sister was also called Maria, followed by Elizabeth, Charlotte, and then himself. With two younger sisters, Emily and Anne, Branwell should have been a middle child.

But, by sheer fortune of his gender, he was often given a preference his sisters were not. That preference came at a price: it was made clear that great things were expected of him. His father had made the journey from Ireland to Cambridge and made something of himself. Branwell was expected to do even better.

Parents and Guardians

But he would have to do it without a mother; Branwell was just four years old when she died. Faced with raising six children by himself, and unable to attract a second wife, Patrick turned to his sister-in-law, Elizabeth Branwell.

'Aunt Branwell' to the children, she moved from temperate Penzance to wind-blasted Haworth to help Patrick take care of her sister's children. Aunt Branwell is often demonised as a strict, hard woman, bitter at being forced to leave her beloved Penzance. Her supposed harsh Christian beliefs are meant to have instilled a varying degree of religious doubt into the Brontë children.

Though this myth has persisted for many years, it is hard to see how. Branwell described Aunt Branwell 'as my mother'[4], an odd thing to say of someone who is meant to have made life mean and miserable. He also wrote that she was 'the guide and director of all the happy days connected with my childhood'[5], which no-one would say of someone who had driven them to the edge of atheism.

Patrick has also been the victim of cruel misrepresentation. Another hard, mean individual according to the myths, he is often said to have shown little affection for the children, and his wild Irish temper was supposedly an inspiration for some of the rougher characters in Brontë fiction. Elizabeth Gaskell seems beside herself with righteous disbelief when she writes of Patrick regularly firing a pistol out of the window.

Yet the reason Patrick had a pistol was a result of one frightening night in Hartshead-cum-Clifton, where he was serving as assistant curate. On the night of 11th April 1812, an army of local Luddites armed with muskets, pistols, hammers and axes passed close to Patrick's home on their way to a bloody, unsuccessful attack on a mill. Undeterred, Luddites attempted to assassinate the mill owner just a week later, and a wool manufacturer was successfully murdered in the same month.

Although Patrick was neither a mill owner nor a wool manufacturer, he admonished the Luddite violence from the pulpit, and likely obtained the pistol from fear of reprisal. The firearm carried just one round, and the only way to remove the bullet was to discharge the weapon daily, rather than leave a loaded gun in a house filled with curious children.

In truth, Patrick appears to have been an attentive father. He would breakfast with the children before giving them morning lessons in his study. His afternoons were spent with his parish, while they were free to walk, play and create their fantasy worlds on the moors. Patrick would return for an evening of talk and further lessons. He was intent on passing on as much of his education as he could, and determined in pursuing every opportunity for his children.

Thus it was that Branwell's sisters, Maria, Elizabeth, Charlotte and Emily were all sent to the Clergy Daughters' School at Cowan Bridge. All of Patrick's girls would need a career to sustain themselves, for the daughters of impoverished clergy were unlikely to attract marriage. Cowan Bridge had been founded specifically to provide for members of the clergy who most needed financial assistance, and raised the spectre of hope that all of the Brontë daughters could receive the education they would need.

Sadly, Cowan Bridge would later become an inspiration for Lowood School in Charlotte's *Jane Eyre*: harsh, mean, and victim of a mismanaged sickness that would claim the life of someone beloved.

The Death of Maria

As the eldest, Maria had taken on elements of the maternal role when their mother had died, and her siblings adored her as they would any mother. Charlotte described her 'prematurely developed and remarkable intellect, as well as ... mildness, wisdom and fortitude'[6] in a letter to her publisher 24 years later, demonstrating just how indelible a mark Maria left on her younger siblings.

Maria developed consumption in December 1824, but the school did not inform Patrick that she was ill until February. It was just a few months later that the disease claimed her life; in May 1825, Maria Brontë died at the age of eleven. Branwell was just seven.

Elizabeth followed just a month later, but it seems that the loss of Maria was the scar that never healed. Charlotte and Emily would write novels in which the majority of characters were orphaned or motherless. Charlotte would admit that the stoic, heroic Helen Burns was inspired by Maria. And Branwell's work would be forever haunted by characters named Maria, Mary, and even Marah, often saintly, often dying. Only Anne was too young to be traumatised by the loss, and she had two older sisters and a brother to adopt Maria's role of mother surrogate.

Childhood Inventions

Patrick fetched home Charlotte and Emily the day after Elizabeth was sent back to Haworth, and kept all four surviving Brontë children at home for the next six years. Patrick's own education came in good stead, allowing him to give his children a classical education which would go on to be a basis for their future literary works.

Further working against the idea that Patrick was a stern, unloving father is a key moment in Brontë lore. In 1826, just one year after the loss of Maria and Elizabeth, Patrick came home with a box of wooden soldiers for Branwell. Charlotte would later recount the episode in a letter, explaining how she snatched up a soldier, declared it her own and named it Wellington. The Duke of Wellington was something of a household hero to the Brontës, and they celebrated the anniversary of the Battle of Waterloo every year. Emboldened by their eldest sister, Emily and Anne claimed a solider of their own. Last but not least, Branwell picked his soldier, and named it Bonaparte.

The children would go on to spin numerous tales around these heroes. Early on they would take a role in their own tales as the Chief Genii, godlike figures with awesome powers, but they soon stepped out of the story and let their heroes take the lead. All four of the children shared this world to begin with, but Emily and Anne soon created their own, private world of Gondal, whilst Charlotte and Branwell set their tales in the fictional African state of Angria.

The inspiration for this setting came from *Blackwood's Magazine*, a monthly journal offering satire and commentary on politics and literature. The long, detailed reviews of biography, history, travel, politics and fiction, replete with extensive quotes, gave the Brontë children access to works that would otherwise be outside their reach. Such was the case with *Mission from Cape Coast Castle to Ashantee*; Blackwood's eighteen page review prompted the Brontë children to set their juvenilia in the African kingdom of Ashantee.

The Brontës had long been putting on plays and acting out fantastical stories in both cellar and moor, but many of these tales were committed to paper in the shape of miniature books filled with tiny script. The children made their tiny books out of whatever scraps they could find, from parcel wrappings to wallpaper. Despite the miniscule size of these volumes, often no bigger than a business card, the writing is neat and precise (albeit so small it can barely be read). These books were also accompanied by a short-lived 'Branwell's Blackwood's Magazine', an outright imitation of the real-life publication.

A Rivalry in Words

Although the children shared their world to begin with, Emily and Anne's partnership soon grew private, leaving Charlotte and Branwell to collaborate alone on their world. But creation was not without its friction. From the moment of conception, Angria was a battlefield between brother and sister.

As the only boy, Branwell was both granted and assumed a higher position in the hierarchy. But Charlotte was still the eldest, and thus had authority of her own. Perhaps it was this conflict between gender and age that was the basis of their rivalry. Perhaps it was simply sibling rivalry, or even just the natural result of the tension needed for good narrative. Whatever the reason, there was as much a war of words as there was peace.

It is nowhere more clear than in the names Charlotte and Branwell chose for their soldiers. Charlotte picked Wellington, national hero, venerated in the Brontë household. Branwell picked Bonaparte, his nemesis. Though the characters evolved, this basic opposition did not. Wellington's mantle was taken up by fictional sons, Arthur and Charles. Bonaparte became Sneaky, then Rogue, and finally Alexander Percy. But Charlotte's characters remained virtuous, handsome and heroic, and Branwell's remained an iconoclast, a demagogue, and a troublemaker.

But it was not just the characters that stood in opposition; the stories themselves were a constant push and pull. When Charlotte's character wrote an accusation of grave robbing and library theft, Branwell wrote an attack in response. When Branwell killed Mary Percy, daughter of Alexander and wife of Arthur, Charlotte attempted to resurrect her. When Charlotte introduced two new aristocratic heroes, Branwell turned them into selfish leaders in a vile Aristocratic Party. Charlotte in turn recast Rogue's dashing buccaneer backstory into a miserable life of exile resulting from a failed attempt to accuse the new characters of treason.

More Than Words

The Brontë children didn't just content themselves with writing their imagined world; they sketched and drew it as well. Charlotte took this artistry further by copying portraits of Lord Byron and those associated with him, illustrating characters from his poems, as well as drawing original landscapes. She nurtured a dream of becoming a professional artist, and in 1834 submitted some of her work for inclusion in the summer exhibition of the Royal Northern Society for the Encouragement of the Arts. Sadly, not one of her pieces was bought, and her dreams were crushed.

The exhibition did begin a new chapter in Branwell's life, however. One of the artists displaying work was William Robinson, an artist with a studio in nearby Leeds. Robinson had studied at the Royal Academy, and been a pupil of Sir Thomas Lawrence, painter-in-ordinary to the King. Patrick was sufficiently impressed to employ him to provide lessons not to Charlotte, but to Branwell.

Under Robinson's tutelage, Branwell produced what would end up being his greatest legacy. The 'Pillar Portrait' hangs today in the National Portrait Gallery in London, depicting Charlotte, Emily, and Anne, and is one of our few contemporary images of them. It hangs alongside a fragment of another family portrait, largely destroyed by Arthur Bell Nichols as he felt the likenesses were terrible save for Emily; her image is all that remains. These two paintings are a huge part of Brontë heritage, and it is a shame that Branwell isn't better appreciated for giving us these portraits.

Yet in the midst of the 'Pillar Portrait' is a pillar through which can be seen a ghostly figure: Branwell himself. The figure is no more than a sketch and was likely abandoned for compositional reasons, but you can make it out because Robinson failed to teach Branwell how to mix his paints properly; the pigments have separated over the years, allowing what was underneath to show through.

Nevertheless, Patrick was clearly pleased enough with Branwell's progress that he drafted a letter to the Royal Academy, asking about the possibility of enrolling his son.

Fact Versus Fiction

The Branwell Myth would now tell you a tale of a boy sent to London to present himself to the Royal Academy, only to waste his money on drink and return home in disgrace, inventing a story about robbery to explain his penniless state.

The truth, however, is that the Royal Academy has no record of any correspondence from either Patrick or Branwell, and neither would have been foolish enough to think an unsolicited visit would endear Branwell to them. The myth appears to be entirely based on one of Branwell's Angrian tales about a character called Charles Wentworth, so overwhelmed by the sights and sounds of the city of Verdopolis that he fails to bear his letters of introduction to their intended recipient. Instead he spends his coin on rum and his time on aimless meandering about the city.

But while writers use their own lives for inspiration, they use other people's lives too and, of course, invent entire people and scenarios from imagination. It's a mistake to read too much into Charles Wentworth, especially as none of the physical evidence supports the myth; Patrick did not send his letter, there is nothing linking Branwell to the Royal Academy, and so we have no reason to invent a tale about a failed trip to London. The plan to attend the Royal Academy was nothing more than an idea, abandoned because it was too costly.

A Father's Support

Nevertheless, Patrick's hopes for his son were undaunted. In an effort to see him well connected, perhaps help him start a career, Patrick enlisted the help of John Brown, the sexton of Haworth and a Master of the Three Graces Lodge, and Joseph Redman, parish clerk and Secretary of the Lodge, to support Branwell's application to the Freemasons.

But at eighteen, Branwell was three years younger than the minimum age of admittance and so, although Brown and Redman had suggested he was 'about 20 Years of Age', his application was rejected. Undeterred, Brown and Redman wrote again, this time describing Branwell as a portrait painter and explaining that he is planning to spend a summer on the continent to pursue further instruction in his art.

This letter appears to have made the difference; Branwell was admitted to the Three Graces Lodge and initiated on 29th February 1836. Branwell's career with the Freemasons outperformed any other career he would enjoy, seeing a promotion to Fellowcraft on 20th April and again to Master Mason just five days later. Yet the trip to the Continent never materialised, presumably for the same reasons he was never sent to London: expense.

It is safe to say that Branwell spent the next two years in Haworth trying to earn a living as a painter. Both Charlotte and Anne were at Roe Head, and although some may enjoy the idea that Branwell was sitting idle in Haworth, it is unlikely that Patrick would have tolerated it. Unfortunately there is little evidence to prove one way or the other what Branwell was doing, save that he attended almost every monthly meeting at the Three Graces Lodge.

What we do know is that he continued to write further Angrian sagas in which the Reform Ministry invaded Angria, placed its people under martial law, and began a reign of terror. Under Branwell's pen, Charlotte's characters Wellington and Zamorna declared war against this regime, whereas Northangerland, having offered secret aid to the Ministry, would later lead a popular revolution to overthrow the regime and place himself at the head of the Provisional Government.

While Branwell was painting portraits and writing Angrian tales, he was also writing to *Blackwood's Magazine*. The publication had been a major influence on all the Brontë children, and Branwell clearly yearned to be a member of its elite group of contributors. His letters speak boldly of his abilities, display little humility, and yet betray his eagerness. His admiration sometimes spills into open flattery, yet he is also stern when he notes he received no reply to his previous letters.

But, despite his determination, Branwell did not receive a single response from *Blackwood's*. Undeterred, he sought a new patron for his work. Charlotte had written to the Poet Laureate, Robert Southey, and received a response. It had been a discouraging response, but it was a response nonetheless. Branwell took it upon himself to write to William Wordsworth.

Branwell paints himself in the best light, offers compliments and flattery, and a plea that Words-worth advise him if he has a future in words. Included with the letter is a poem, 'Still and bright, in twilight shining'. The poem is Branwell's most Wordsworthian work, perhaps chosen to further flatter the man. Unfortunately, Wordsworth was reportedly unimpressed with the letter, and never sent a reply.

But whereas Charlotte allowed Southey's discouragement to temporarily cease her love affair with letters, Branwell forged ahead. On 9th March 1837 he began to collect his best poems, going back as far as 1833, and then corrected and transcribed them into a new note-book. He would go on to add more recent compositions to this note-book, and some of the contents would inspire his future efforts at publication.

A Career in Politics

Branwell also became a political figure that year. On 27th January he established a Haworth Operative Conservative Society, the objectives of which were to 'maintain loyalty to the King attachment to the connection between church and State respect for the independence and prerogatives of the House of Lords and a proper regard for the Commons House of Parliament'[7].

Given how much Branwell enjoyed writing Angrian tales about Alexander Percy, Earl of Northangerland and political demagogue, it is interesting to see his real-world affection for the status quo.

That being said, 1837 did see Branwell, and Patrick too, in opposition to the government of the day. The Poor Law Amendment Act of 1834 was just beginning to take effect in Yorkshire, and saw anyone unfit to work being put into the workhouses. There the men, women, and children were separated and expected to perform hard, back-breaking labour to earn their keep. With so many advancements in the textile trade, many workers in Yorkshire found themselves faced with the choice between splitting up their family or risking starvation together.

Patrick was vocal in his opposition, calling a meeting to petition Parliament to repeal the Poor Law Amendment Act. The meeting was so well attended it had to be held outside, where Patrick urged the whole village to oppose the Act, even mentioning rebellion (albeit as a possible, undesirable consequence of the deprivation inflicted by the Act).

It was Branwell who read and moved the petition, and the support was unanimous. But such support wasn't a regular feature of Branwell's short-lived political career. Just five days later, a meeting was held to petition Parliament again, this time to abolish church rates. These were effectively a tax that went to the upkeep of parish churches. Patrick and Branwell opposed abolition of the rates; they both knew how much parish churches relied on the money the rates brought in.

But the Brontë men were in the minority; not everyone was so willing to make compulsory contributions to one church in favour of another. For example, Hall Green Baptist Chapel, where the meeting was held, didn't benefit from church rates, and nor did any Roman Catholic churches.

Patrick and Branwell found themselves vilified for their opposition to the petition, and Branwell was even accused of sending false statements to the newspapers. There isn't any evidence that he did so, and Juliet Barker believes the accuser had confused Branwell with William Hodgson, Patrick's curate, who had indeed written to a newspaper about church rates.

It wouldn't be the last time that Branwell would be so vilified. Just a few months later, Parliament was dissolved in the wake of King William IV's death in June 1837. When the Whig candidate, Lord Morpeth, visited Haworth to speak to his electorate, Patrick tried to ask him some questions. But Patrick was a know Tory, despite his opposition to the Poor Law Amendment Act, and the crowd overwhelmingly supported the Whigs. They shouted him down, prompting Branwell to step forward and declare 'If you won't let my father speak, you shan't speak.'[8]

Noble, perhaps, but fruitless. Lord Morpeth was elected, and Branwell faced the indignity of seeing his effigy carried down the street and then burnt. At least he could claim a dramatic end to his political career.

Stepping into the World

Despite Branwell's tutelage with William Robinson, Patrick seems to have had doubts that his son had a future in paint. He wrote to John Driver, a merchant and a banker in Liverpool, confessing that he has considered many options for Branwell (painting is not listed as one of them), including merchant trades and a university education. Patrick felt the former required introductions that were hard to come by, and the latter was too expensive. Instead he raised the possibility of working as a banking clerk, with the chance for progression and success once a foot was in the door, and asked Driver for his help. Unfortunately, Driver was either unwilling or unable to help with the necessary introductions, and so painting was decided upon as a last resort.

Thus it was that Branwell was set up as a portrait painter in the nearby city of Bradford by the end of July that year. This was possible only with the assistance of Reverend William Morgan, an old friend Patrick had made while he had been assistant curate in Wellington, Shropshire. By 1837, Morgan was based in Bradford and able to help Branwell find lodgings with a man called Isaac Kirby, who had a commercial premises in the city from which he sold beer.

Some like to suggest that Branwell was already a hardened drinker at this point, citing many scenes of drunken debauchery in his Angrian stories as evidence. Aside from the fact he and Charlotte had been writing such scenes since they were children, inspired by their reading habits, it hardly seems likely that Patrick would have allowed Branwell to lodge with a dealer of beer if he was a drinker.

Branwell painted portraits of William Morgan, Isaac Kirby and his family, and the vicar of Bradford himself, Henry Heap. But Branwell's time in Bradford was to be short-lived; Angrian stories dated from Haworth, letters sent to contacts in Bradford, and other notes and footnotes in Haworth suggest he returned home after just six months.

First Failures

The Branwell Myth would have you believe that Branwell's failure was down to drink, debauchery, and delinquency. Branwell certainly admitted to having certain debts which he could not confess to his father or aunt, which might suggest they were to do with drink.

But there is no evidence that Branwell fell into a squalor of drink and drugs. It is far more likely that he simply lived beyond his means, a mistake many young men and women make at some point in their lives, particularly when living away from their family for the first time. This is backed up by testimony from his landlord's niece, who describes Branwell as 'a very steady young gentleman'[9].

If drink and debt wasn't the source of Branwell's failure, what was? Put simply, he wasn't talented enough. Bradford was a competitive place for a portrait painter, made worse by the fact that both nearby Halifax and Leeds were also full of both aspiring and established painters. Branwell's skill with a brush was just not enough to gain him notice, and he failed to garner enough commissions to support himself. The difficulties of earning a living as a painter were made clear by the unexpected death of William Robinson, Branwell's tutor, who died at the age of just thirty-nine. Despite being a Royal Academian and pupil of Thomas Lawrence, Robinson had earnt so little that he left nothing for his wife and children. It is therefore no surprise that Branwell failed.

Branwell's return to Haworth was not unique amongst his siblings. All three of his sisters had similarly ventured forth into the world only to return. Over three years from 1835 to 1838, Charlotte, Emily, and Anne had all left home for Roe Head school, where Charlotte had received her education after the tragedies at Cowan Bridge She had returned to Roe Head in 1835 to work as a governess, and Emily went with her to attend the school as a student. Emily had lasted just three months before home-sickness brought on real illness and forced her return. Anne took Emily's place, and lasted two years before a religious crisis brought on her own illness. Finally, having struggled with unhappiness and frustration for almost three years, Charlotte finally gave up her employment and returned home.

With her characteristic quiet determination, Anne was the first to find new employment, but Branwell wasn't far behind, responding to an advert in the *Leeds Intelligencer* seeking a tutor. The post was in the Lake District, then something of a haven for poets. It must have seemed to Branwell the perfect opportunity to not only make his way in the world, but to also perhaps further his career in letters.

The Beginnings of the Poet

Branwell's new employer was Robert Postlethwaite, a prominent landowner in the Lake District, and Branwell was to provide his sons with a classical education. Branwell lodged, not with Postlethwaite, but with another family in the town of Broughton. Edward Fish, his landlord, was described by Branwell as a drunk, his wife as a kind-hearted soul, and of his pretty daughter Margaret, Branwell would say very little.

Branwell did write of other pretty young women, though, in one of a handful of letters to John Brown. Brown was the sexton of Haworth, responsible for maintaining the church and its grounds, including the graveyard. His daughter, Martha, had moved into the parsonage to help with the running of the household, and Brown had become firm friends with Branwell. In all their correspondence, there is a sense that Branwell is trying to impress Brown. Perhaps because Brown was thirteen years older, perhaps because he was respected as a Master of the Three Graces Lodge, perhaps because he was partly responsible for making Branwell's application to the Lodge a success. Whatever the reason, there is an almost overbearing feeling of bravado when Branwell addresses Brown as 'the Old Knave of Trumps' and writes:

> as to the young ones! – I have one sitting by me just now – fair-faced, blue eyes, dark haired sweet eighteen – she little thinks the devil is so near her![10]

But while there was a degree of freedom in not living with his employer, it seems that Branwell used it for pursuits that were more gentlemanly than devilish. He took full advantage of living in the Lake District, walking along the River Duddon with a copy of Wordsworth's sonnets in hand, inspired enough by the scenery to pen 'Black Comb'. Written about the mountain of the same name opposite the Duddon estuary, 'Black Comb' would go on to be one of the best of Branwell's published poems.

He also turned his mind to seeking out local talent for encouragement and advice. He reworked a poem he had written in Bradford, renaming it 'Sir Henry Tunstall', and sent it, along with his translation of some of Horace's *Odes*, to Thomas de Quincey. De Quincey was the infamous writer of *Confessions of an Opium Eater*, and a contributor to *Blackwood's Magazine*. De Quincey kept the manuscript of Branwell's *Odes*, but was ill at the time of Branwell's letter; there is no evidence that he replied.

Just five days after writing to De Quincey, Branwell wrote to another local poet. Branwell sent 300 lines of poetry to Hartley Coleridge, son of Samuel Taylor Coleridge, as well as some translations of the *Odes*. His letter was rather more temperate than those he had written to *Blackwood's* or Wordsworth, and this temperance was to reward him. Hartley wrote back.

Branwell spent a day with Hartley at his home and, although we don't have any details of their meeting, it was clearly a great inspiration to Branwell. He immediately began work on the rest of his translation of Horace's *Odes*, which Hartley promised to read.

But Branwell's enthusiasm for his new place in the Lake District was to be cut short. Less than two months after he met Hartley Coleridge, Robert Postlethwaite dismissed him from his post.

Father Branwell?

There are different theories as to why Branwell was dismissed. We will probably never know for certain. Some suggest he was so inspired by Hartley's encouragement that he neglected his education of Postlethwaite's children. Others suggest that he turned up to Postlethwaite's home one day both late and drunk. There is also a suggestion that Branwell fathered an illegitimate child on one of Postlethwaite's servants.

Once again, these claims appear to have their basis in Branwell's work, this time a poem written in 1846 called 'Letter From a Father on Earth to His Child in Her Grave'. This, many claim, suggests that Branwell fathered a child that died young, and the most likely time he could have done this was whilst working for Postlethwaite.

After the error involving Charles Wentworth and the Royal Academy, it would be easy to dismiss this as another instance of confusing a writer's work with autobiography. But Juliet Barker's excellent biography, *The Brontës*, suggests there is something to this story.

A friend of Elizabeth Gaskell, Richard Monckton Milnes, claimed in 1859 that Branwell sired an illegitimate child whilst working for Robert Postlethwaite. He suggested this was the reason Branwell was dismissed after a mere six months in the post, and that the child later died. He also claimed that John Brown verbally confirmed the tale.

Barker has looked up the illegitimate children recorded in the parish at the time. Two of them aren't viable candidates, but one, Mary born to Agnes Riley, seems to fit the bill. Mary was born in February 1841, putting the conception at May 1840, while Branwell was still in Postlethwaite's employ. This also gives the pregnancy enough time to be confirmed by the time Branwell was dismissed. And we only have to look at Branwell's work to see how much he favoured the name 'Mary'; is this all too much a coincidence?

It was originally thought that there were no records of Mary after

June 1841, and it was assumed that she had died young, which would fit the theory nicely. But Sarah Elizabeth Griffiths uncovered records of a Mary Riley up until a register of burials in December 1868.[11]

If this Mary Riley is the right one (it isn't always easy to be sure), this throws a question on the root of the entire theory: Branwell wrote a poem from a father to his dead child, but Mary was alive and well when he wrote it. Either Branwell was laboring under the impression Mary had died, or he was writing metaphorically. There is no evidence of any correspondence between him and Agnes; perhaps he felt Mary was dead to him in all the ways that mattered.

Unless, of course, Branwell didn't father any children; we must be careful not to assume truth where there is only conjecture. The lack of correspondence, indeed any link, between Branwell and Agnes makes this all guesswork. And there isn't anyone else to corroborate the claim. Branwell might have hidden the truth out of shame, and destroyed any correspondence. But the only facts we have are that Branwell was in the same parish as Agnes Riley when her daughter was conceived, and that, six years later, he wrote a poem from the perspective of a father speaking to his dead child. And these facts are arranged to support a testimony from a friend of Elizabeth Gaskell, whose own bias is well-established.

Railway Man

Whatever the reason, Branwell spent just six months in his post with the Postlethwaites. But his dismissal did not dampen his literary ambitions. Within two days of his return to Haworth, he had polished further work on Horace's *Odes* and sent it to Hartley.

Unfortunately, although a draft of Hartley's response exists, it was never sent. Had Branwell received these words, perhaps they would have given him the encouragement and motivation to pursue his dream with more determination.

> I was struck with the power and energy of the lines you sent before I had the pleasure of seeing you. Your translation of Horace is a work

> of much greater promise, and though I do not counsel a publication of the whole – I think many odes might appear with very little alteration. Your versification is often masterly – and you have shown skill in great variety of measures[12]

While Branwell waited for a response that would never come, he began to take a great interest in the new railway being built between Leeds and Manchester. This new and exciting technology caught Branwell's imagination and, when there came an opportunity to work at one of the new stations, he leapt at the chance.

The post of assistant clerk-in-charge at Sowerby Bridge station paid just £75 a year, much less than he could earn as a tutor. But with annual pay rises and the possibility of promotion, his prospects were better. Nevertheless, Charlotte made fun of Branwell's appointment, sarcastically describing his new post as 'adventurous, romantic, knight-errant-like'[13] despite the fact that she had made no attempt to find a new job since she had left Roe Head.

The new railway opened in October 1840 and, although the job itself would have kept Branwell busy, the chief benefit was that Sowerby Bridge was just four miles from Halifax. The musical, literary, and artistic circles the city offered would have been a siren's call to Branwell, and it was also home to an old friend, Joseph Leyland, who Branwell had known in Bradford.

Branwell flourished in his new role. After just six months, he was promoted to clerk-in-charge further up the line at Luddenden Foot station. He received a much higher salary in this post, £130 a year, but Charlotte remained unimpressed. She believed her younger brother should have been a writer or an artist, and his current role was all-too mundane for him. Or perhaps her own working life was too mundane for her; she had been unhappy at Roe Head, and perhaps was transferring some of her dissatisfaction with her own life onto her brother.

It was at Luddenden Foot that Branwell met Francis Grundy, who was a fellow worker on the railway. Writing about Branwell years later, Grundy painted a grim picture of Luddenden Foot as an isolated backwater that drove Branwell 'to the bad'[14] through boredom. Grundy's story went unquestioned for years, but it was just not true. There was a village close to the station, and Branwell is known to have visited Manchester using the free travel he was permitted as a railway employee. With access to plenty of diversions, as well as good pay and excellent prospects, there is no reason or evidence to think this posting drove Branwell to drink and ruin.

In fact, the opposite seems to be true, for Branwell's writing at this time shows a degree of care and craft that was previously lacking. While his work as a younger man showed a breathless, even sloppy enthusiasm, his poetry at this time benefitted from constant revisions and a search for the perfect turn of phrase. It is no coincidence that Branwell saw his first poem, 'Heaven and Earth', published in the *Halifax Guardian* in June, just one month after his promotion to Luddenden Foot.

Successful Poet

The fact that Branwell was both a published poet, and also published five years before his sisters, is somehow little known and also quickly dismissed. It probably didn't help that Branwell didn't publish under his own name. Instead he used the pseudonym Northangerland, taken from his Angrian stories; Alexander Percy, Branwell's favourite character, was Earl of Northangerland.

Branwell's detractors also like to point out that he was published in newspapers, as if this was somehow a lesser achievement. They also like to suggest that he made use of his friendship with Joseph Leyland to secure publication of unworthy poetry.

Yet the *Halifax Guardian* published poetry from many well-known poets, and didn't hesitate to reject submissions it thought were unworthy of publication. And, although Joseph Leyland's father had printed and published the *Halifax Guardian* until 1837, the paper was under new authority by the time Branwell was published.

It's more likely that these are cheap attempts to undermine Branwell's achievements in favour of the Branwell Myth. The truth is that

Branwell's poetry was not only published before his sisters', but it was better received. This can be true without dimming the light of Charlotte, Emily, or Anne, and therefore there is no reason to take the light away from Branwell.

Branwell had one other poem published during his time at Luddenden Foot, and this was the only poem ever published under his own name. 'On the Melbourne Ministry' celebrated the fall of the Whig government and the return to power of the Conservatives. Short, political, and contemporary, it stands apart from the rest of his work and, considering his previous political career in Haworth, this might explain why he did not attach it to his pseudonym.

But Branwell produced more than these two poems during this time. His notebooks are filled with new compositions and new versions of previous efforts. It was a time of great production and great prospects, and so it is a shame that it was cut short by his sudden dismissal from the railways.

Another Job Lost

An audit of the station ledgers in March 1842 showed disarray, as well as a shortfall of £11 1s. 7d. The Branwell Myth would have you believe Branwell spent the company money on drink, but it is, again, a claim with no substance to it. The railways were known for their harsh attitude to wrong-doing, even going so far as to prosecute and seek prison sentences. Branwell, however, was faced only with dismissal. The fact that Grundy tried to help him find work for the railway again suggests that re-employment was possible, therefore making Branwell's transgression relatively minor.

The likely truth is that Branwell left the bookkeeping to an underling, and was deemed responsible for the error, whatever the reason behind it. After all, Branwell was in charge; if an underling mislaid (or misappropriated) money, Branwell had to face the consequences of delegating a responsibility to the wrong person.

Branwell wrote to Grundy 22nd May, telling his friend that the return to Haworth was accompanied by illness, misery, depression and drink. The facts, however, suggest that Branwell was exaggerating and perhaps even looking for sympathy. The truth is that, while Branwell might have been anxious about his father's and aunt's reaction to his dismissal, any anxiety did not last long.

He certainly felt confident enough to recommend his old friend, Joseph Leyland, to sculpt a memorial to the recently deceased Haworth surgeon. And the time following his dismissal marked the most productive literary period Branwell ever enjoyed.

Less than a month after he was dismissed from Luddenden Foot, Branwell saw his poem 'On Landseer's Painting' published in the new Tory newspaper, the *Bradford Herald*. 'On the Callousness produced by Cares' was published in both the *Bradford Herald* and *Halifax Guardian* just a week later. This was followed by 'The Afghan War', 'On Peaceful Death and Painful Life', 'Caroline's Prayer', 'Song', 'An Epicurean's Song', 'On Caroline', and 'Noah's Warning over Methuselah's Grave', all in the space of four months.

On top of publication, Branwell was reaching out to the literary world again. He sent his work to: James Montgomery, a poet based in Sheffield; Caroline Bowles, wife of Robert Southey and poet in her own right; Leigh Hunt, essayist and editor of the *Examiner*; and, via Grundy, Harriet Martineau, an author of novels.

With varying degrees of positive responses and encouragement from these literary bastions, he perhaps felt optimistic in writing again to *Blackwood's Magazine*. This time he wrote a sober, considered, and less egotistical letter, drafting it first before making a neat copy, demonstrating how much he had matured since his last letter. Unfortunately, despite the improvement in his attitude and approach, he still didn't receive a response.

Worse, October 1842 saw the loss of, in his words, one who had been as a mother. Aunt Branwell fell suddenly ill with an intestinal obstruction. Someone afflicted with this painful condition suffers from dehydration, shock, and even death without intravenous fluids and possible surgery. Neither was available to Aunt Branwell, who endured days of agony before she passed away at the age of 66. Her death struck Branwell deeply, and when he wrote to Grundy to pass on the news, he described it as the loss of 'the guide and and director of all the happy days connected with my childhood'[15].

The loss of Aunt Branwell brought all the Brontë children home, Charlotte and Emily from Brussels where they had been studying at the Pensionnat Heger, Anne from her position as governess to the Robinsons at Thorp Green. All four of them remained in the parsonage until 27th January 1843 saw Charlotte return to Brussels. Emily did not go with her; she remained to take up the running of the household, while Anne and Branwell set off for Thorp Green together. Branwell had a job again.

Doomed Tutor

Reverend Edmund Robinson was a wealthy clergyman. Husband to his wife, Lydia, and father to five children, Robinson was chronically ill and rarely officiated any more. Nevertheless, he maintained a grand estate at Thorp Green which was tended to by ten live-in servants.

By the end of 1843, Anne had been tutoring four of the five Robinson children for almost three years. Although she had considered leaving on occasion, she had won the Robinsons' regard and they pleaded with her to stay, so she did. And when she suggested her brother as a tutor for Edmund Robinson, who had outgrown her care, the Robinsons were happy to accept her recommendation.

The change in station seems to have been difficult for Branwell to adapt to. After the independence he had enjoyed working on the railway, the post of tutor must have seemed much more of a restriction. He was cut off from his friends and his family; he didn't even share a roof with Anne, sleeping instead in separate lodgings. It seems Branwell was initially so miserable he became ill, and Patrick was concerned enough that he visited his son while making a trip to York.

Nevertheless, the Robinsons appreciated Branwell's skills, and it was not long until he was settled into his new post. Anne attests that the two of them were greatly appreciated by the Robinsons. Branwell also continued his literary efforts. Lydia Robinson was distantly related to Thomas Babington Macaulay, who had written the highly regarded *Lays of Ancient Rome* in 1842. Through Mrs Robinson, Branwell received a complimentary letter from Macaulay; it seems she encouraged Branwell's poetic efforts, while Mr Robinson dismissed them out of hand.

Branwell also had four poems published in a new outlet, the *Yorkshire Gazette*. Two were old poems, 'Black Comb' and 'On Landseer's Picture', the others a pair of sonnets under the title 'The Emigrant'. The subject matter was timely given the number of emigrations of the period; poverty and hunger had driven many families from England to find fuller plates in Canada, Australia, and New Zealand.

Sadly, and just as before, a period of poetic energy was swiftly followed by dismissal.

The Beginning of the End

Branwell was dismissed from Thorp Green in July 1845. The precise reason why has never been established, and baseless accusations have ranged from theft to sexual abuse of his young charge. But the most popular theory, and one espoused by Branwell himself, is that he engaged in an affair with Lydia Robinson, his employer's wife.

This was Branwell's explanation, and one he repeated many times. He began telling his tale as early as May 1843, just a few months into his new position, with a letter to John Brown. This is the same John Brown he wrote to whilst in the Postlethwaite's employ, bragging that the pretty young ladies do not suspect he is a devil. But this time the lady is seventeen years his senior, and 'DAMNABLY TOO FOND OF ME'[16]. Branwell suggests that Lydia offers him gifts, and asks Brown if he should return her favours with his own.

Lord Houghton, who ostensibly provided the story that Branwell fathered an illegitimate child in Broughton, summarises another letter from Branwell to Brown. In November 1843, Branwell claims Mrs Robinson is 'his lady'[17], and describes the agony of not having her lying with him at night. He also writes that a member of the

Robinson's staff had caught him in an act with Lydia Robinson that would see him hanged if it ever came to light.

Charlotte would report that Branwell was irritable when he was at home in Haworth, and mentioned to Monsieur Heger that he was often ill. But there was no great upset until 1845, and no indication of the storm that was to break.

Anne handed in her notice and left the Robinsons' employ in June. There isn't much evidence as to why Anne left. She had considered it in the past but either the Robinsons or Anne's sense of duty to her family (as the only consistent bread-winner) had persuaded her to stay. Something had finally changed her mind, but whether she saw the writing on the wall, or had simply had enough of the Robinsons, she never committed the reason to paper.

Branwell remained with the Robinsons despite Anne's resignation. He spent a week in Haworth in June, returning to the Robinsons until they went on holiday to Scarborough. Branwell returned home and, just weeks later, received his letter of dismissal.

We don't know the exact contents of the letter, only Charlotte's description, which came to her via Anne. According to Charlotte, Mr Robinson had called Branwell's conduct as 'bad beyond expression' and forbade any further contact with his family 'on pain of exposure'[18]. Branwell claimed this bad conduct described his affair with Lydia Robinson, and also told people that Mr Robinson had threatened to shoot him should he go near the family again.

Either way, Branwell was unemployed again. The question we are left with is: what did he do that was bad beyond expression? To get into the details would derail this biography, so I have addressed this question in the next chapter.

For now, all we need to know is that the story of Branwell's affair was largely accepted by his friends and family. If we are to believe Charlotte, we are to think that Branwell descended into intolerable behavior, drowning his sorrows and making life a misery at the parsonage. But we must remember that Charlotte's testimony is also unreliable. Her scathing descriptions of Branwell are filled with a sense of injustice, presumably because she is guilty of similar sins:

she longed after Monsieur Heger, a married man, and her letters to him are filled with as much overwrought angst as Branwell. I suggested that Charlotte's sarcasm and cruel jibes towards Branwell's work on the railway was a way of transferring some of her dissatisfaction with herself onto her brother; I suggest she did the same when it came to an extra-marital affair, whether actual or desired.

So when she complains that Branwell makes no attempt to find employment, it reads on the surface as if Branwell has become a selfish burden. It reads differently when you remember that Charlotte had made no attempt to find employment for two years. And, in the end, it was untrue. Branwell had written to Grundy a number of times enquiring about another job on the railway, even considering a post on the continent if he could not get one in England.

And rather than languishing in a pit of despair, drink, and drugs as the Branwell Myth would have you believe, Branwell was in fact quite active after his dismissal. Certainly he was depressed – no more than Charlotte about her own lost love – but he published two new poems towards the end of 1845, 'Real Rest' and 'Penmaenmawr', both inspired by his time with Mrs Robinson. He also considered writing again to *Blackwood's Magazine*, drafting but never sending the letter; perhaps this was not the time for another silent refusal.

This was also a time of innovation for Branwell, for he attempted something new that even his sisters had not yet embarked on: a novel. Branwell described his new project to Leyland in September 1845 as having less to do with inspiration and more to do with money:

> in the present state of the publishing and reading world a Novel is the most saleable article so that where ten pounds would be offered for a work the production of which would require the utmost stretch of a man's intellect – two hundred pounds would be a refused offer for three volumes whose composition would require the smoking of a cigar and the humming of a tune.[19]

Clearly Branwell had heard somewhere that a novel could command a greater payment than a poem, and this might have encouraged him to a new, mercenary attitude towards writing. After all, he was now 28, with no professional or personal prospects on the horizon. If he was going to be a man of letters, he would need to accelerate the process, so he turned to an unfinished Angrian story. Begun in 1837, it had told the tale of a young Alexander Percy and his seduction of a married woman. It's not surprising that Branwell returned to this subject material, relocating it to England's shores but leaving the characters unchanged, perhaps to faster finish his project. But he never did; perhaps Branwell realised it wasn't as easy to write a novel after all.

But while Branwell's novel went unpublished, his public declaration of intent had certainly influenced Charlotte to put together a volume of poetry for publication. Given that Charlotte thought Branwell wasn't making an effort to find a job, and had no idea he was a published poet, it isn't surprising that she didn't include him in the venture. In fact she would later claim that he never knew of any of their publications. But with packages of manuscripts and advance proofs flying in and out of the parsonage, there is no chance that Branwell didn't know what his sisters were up to.

The knowledge that he had been excluded would have left him feeling alienated, lonely, and possibly something of a failure. All of his life he had been told he should aspire to great things. Now his sisters were publishing a book of poetry, and doing it without him. He likely had no idea that they were paying for it all out of their own pocket, but even that fact would have been a poor comfort.

Charlotte, Emily and Anne should not be blamed for excluding Branwell, and there is no sense in thinking about what might have been. But I suspect that had they known of his success, and included him in their efforts, we would have celebrated four Brontës instead of three.

But it's easy to forgive the sisters for giving Branwell wide berth. Despite a burst of creativity, he had never quite recovered from his unexpected dismissal. He had begun to drink regularly, and was perhaps even taking opium at this point. He described his state in a letter to Leyland in April 1846:

> when I fall back on myself I suffer so much wretchedness that I cannot withstand any temptations to get out of myself[20]

The desire for escape has encouraged many addictions and will encourage many more. Nevertheless, Branwell kept himself busy. He composed a poem about the uprisings in India and spent three days in Halifax with an old acquaintance, John Frobisher, the organist at the Halifax Parish Church, to discuss setting it to music. Whilst there he placed an advert in the *Halifax Guardian* seeking employment and, when he returned, he took up his pen and wrote the poem that raised so much speculation about his possible parenthood: 'Letter From a Father on Earth to His Child in Her Grave'.

He also embarked on a project at the behest of his friend, Joseph Leyland: Branwell would write an epic poem detailing the history of Morley Hall in Lancashire, and Leyland would sculpt a portrait of Branwell in return. Though some of Branwell's work exists, it is unfinished, but Leyland's medallion portrait is one of the few images we have of Branwell today.

In the midst of this activity arrived *Poems*, the fruits of Charlotte's, Emily's, and Anne's labours. Branwell is certain to have seen the finished article. Perhaps he was pleased for his sisters. It would be nice to think so. But it was undoubtedly hard for him to see the results of the efforts he had been excluded from. But if it was a blow to see *Poems*, it could not compare to what was coming next.

Mr Robinson died 26th May 1846, leaving Lydia Robinson a widow. Branwell was ecstatic at the thought of reunion and, incidentally, becoming a gentleman of leisure in the process.

> I had reason to hope that ere very long I should be the husband of a Lady whom I loved best in the world and with whom, in more than competence, I might live at leisure to try to make myself a name in the world of posterity, without being pestered by the small but countless botherments, which like mosquitoes sting us in the world of work-day toil.[21]

But Branwell's hopes, both romantic and financial, were about to be permanently dashed.

The Final Blow

A letter written by Charlotte describes the news that Mr Robinson had altered his will, stipulating that his widow would be left penniless if she reopened communication with Branwell. Although this is the story that Branwell repeatedly told to family and friends, it isn't true; Mr Robinson made no such alteration to his will.

Some have suggested that there was no affair to begin with, and Branwell invented the tale to explain why he didn't marry Lydia Robinson. Others suggest that Lydia herself told the lie to keep Branwell at bay.

I'll go into more detail in the next chapter. For now, all that matters is that the lie was believed. Branwell made his heartbreak and hopelessness plain to anyone who would listen.

> Noble writings, works of art, music or poetry now instead of rousing my imagination, cause a whirlwind of blighting sorrow that sweeps over my mind with unspeakable dreariness.[22]

Alienated from his family and divorced from his dreams, Branwell spent a lot of time in Halifax, even lodging for a time at a public house. But he had no means to finance this lifestyle, resulting in a visit to the parsonage from a sheriff's officer demanding payment of debts incurred. Even after this debt was paid, Branwell's letters reveal he was worried about other unpaid bills.

This certainly wasn't helped by receiving two letters from Thorp Green. The first came from Dr Crosby, the medical attendant to the Robinson family, returning a letter Branwell had written to Lydia, unopened. The second came Ann Marshall, Lydia's lady's-maid, telling Branwell that her mistress was on the brink of hysteria and madness from being forced by her late husband's will to remain apart from him.

The idea that Lydia was suffering and that they would be forever parted saw him sink into an even deeper depression than before. If it was escape he had sought before, now he sought oblivion, a search made easier by sums of money sent to him by Lydia. Branwell was worried about his drinking, but not in the way you might expect. He feared that, like his Angrian anti-hero Northangerland, his constitution could handle any binge and would 'keep me years in torture and despair when I should every hour pray that I might die'[23].

As Weak As Man

Northangerland, though, had the benefit of being fictional; Branwell was all too mortal, and the constant assault of drink and drugs weakened his body until he became ill. After drinking away a considerable sum of money from Lydia, and finding himself the unwilling beneficiary of sobriety, Branwell suffered a fit which was just the beginning of delirium tremens. Often caused by alcohol withdrawal, delirium tremens subjects the victim to shaking, shivering, sweating, hallucinations and even seizures.

Forced by poverty and health to avoid drink, he turned instead to his writing, reworking an old Angrian poem of misery and death that he titled 'End of All' and sent to the *Halifax Guardian*.

But where success had once encouraged a burst of creativity in Branwell, there was no such burst this time. Instead he drank what he could spend, and was ill when he couldn't drink. He tried to cover up his illness in a letter to Leyland, blaming his broken heart for his fainting fits. But it wasn't a broken heart that set his bed sheets on fire.

It was pragmatic Emily who saved Branwell from the blaze, throwing the burning sheets into the middle of the room and dousing them with water. Branwell would sleep in his father's room after that night, but even this humiliation wasn't enough to stir Branwell to right himself. Instead he continued to request and receive money from Lydia Robinson and, when he had this money, he drank it. When he didn't, he drank lines of credit and promises of future payment. Neither of these were infinite wells, and Branwell often faced demands for settlement and even threats of court summons. This left him spending his money on his debts, and simply raising new debts to pay for that night's drinking.

He was in such a sorry state that he was reduced to begging John Brown for five pence of gin to be delivered to him while his family was at church, promising to pay him out of a gift of a shilling, likely to be begged from his father after the service was over.

The End of Branwell Brontë

The drunkenness, the hangovers, the stress caused by debt, and the heartache was taking its toll. Delerium tremens had taken firm hold, as well as bouts of influenza, both serving to mask a much deeper problem: consumption, which we know today as tuberculosis.

A bacterial infection of the lungs that causes bloody coughing, fever, and weight loss (which is why it used to be called 'consumption'), tuberculosis is less of a threat these days thanks to improved sanitation and vaccination. But both were in short supply in 1840s Haworth. The infection had already claimed Branwell's older sisters, Maria and Elizabeth, and it would go on to claim Emily and Anne after it was done with Branwell.

So, although the testimony of Francis Grundy should always be taken with a generous pinch of salt, it's easy to believe that, when he surprised Branwell with dinner in the Black Bull, Branwell arrived with

> unkempt, uncut hair...cheeks yellow and hollow, the mouth fallen, the thin white lips not trembling but shaking, the sunken eyes, once small, now glaring with the light of madness[24]

(It is less easy to believe, however, that Branwell had thought the invitation come from Satan and had come to dinner armed with a knife.)

It was shortly after this visit, though, that Branwell quickly declined. After a walk into the village, he was so weak and short of breath that he struggled over the step back into the parsonage. The next day he couldn't get out of bed, and a doctor proclaimed him close to death. Though Branwell's spirits were calmer, the bleakness cannot have entirely left him, as it was on this day he uttered the words that have hounded him since: 'In all my past life I have done nothing either great or good.'[25] We know that to be untrue, but his family did not.

Branwell died in his father's bed on Sunday 24th September 1848 at the age of just 31. He did not clamber to his feet to prove a man could die standing; that's just another of Gaskell's fictions. He died on his back, surrounded by his family, with prayers on his lips.

He was buried on Thursday 28th September in the family vault, alongside his mother, Maria, and his sisters, Maria and Elizabeth.

Meeting Branwell Brontë

A writer's story is as much in their words as it is in the facts of their life, and such is the case with Branwell Brontë. I mentioned that the question of his relationship with Lydia Robinson would derail his biography. That was true, but there is another figure that needs to be introduced before I can explain what probably happened at Thorp Green. To decide whether or not Branwell had an affair with Lydia Robinson, and to understand why no-one knew he was a published poet, I will need to introduce you to Branwell's chief creation: Alexander Percy, Earl of Northangerland.

---

1. Juliet Barker, *The Brontës: A Life in Letters* (Viking, 1997) p. 209
2. Juliet Barker, *The Brontës: A Life in Letters* (Viking, 1997) p. 179
3. Juliet Barker, *The Brontës: A Life in Letters* (Viking, 1997) p. 179
4. Letter 18
5. Letter 19
6. Juliet Barker, *The Brontës: A Life in Letters* (Viking, 1997) p. 9

7. Victor A. Neufeldt, *The Works of Patrick Branwell Brontë* (Garland Publishing, 1999) p. 21
8. Juliet Barker, *The Brontës* (Abacus, 2010) p. 314
9. Winnifred Gerin, *Branwell Brontë: A Biography* (Hutchinson & Co, 1972) p. 142
10. Letter 8
11. Sarah Elizabeth Griffiths, 'Branwell Brontë, Agnes and Mary Riley', *Brontë Studies* (Vol. 36 No. 4, November 2011) p. 358-62
12. Letter 11
13. Juliet Barker, *The Brontës: A Life in Letters* (Viking, 1997) p. 81
14. Francis Grundy, *Pictures of the Past : Memories of Men I have Met and Places I have Seen* (Griffith and Faran, 1879) p. 75
15. Letter 19
16. Letter 20
17. Juliet Barker, *The Brontës* (Abacus, 2010) p. 544
18. Juliet Barker, *The Brontës: A Life in Letters* (Viking, 1997) p. 134
19. Letter 24
20. Letter 29
21. Letter 36
22. Letter 36
23. Letter 36
24. Francis Grundy, *Pictures of the Past : Memories of Men I have Met and Places I have Seen* (Griffith and Faran, 1879) p. 91
25. Juliet Barker, *The Brontës: A Life in Letters* (Viking, 1997) p. 208

WHO IS ALEXANDER PERCY?

WHEN PATRICK BRONTË BROUGHT HOME A BOX OF WOODEN SOLDIERS IN 1826, his children took one each and gave it a name. Branwell named his Bonaparte, but that wasn't a name that would last in a household that idolised the Duke of Wellington. Branwell changed his soldier's name to Sneaky, then Alexander Rogue, before finally settling on Alexander Percy. Percy would stay with Branwell for the rest of his life. Although he wrote about other characters in Angria, even adopted them as favourites for a time, it was always Percy that Branwell returned to.

It isn't hard to see why; Percy would have been fun to write. He was the epitome of a Byronic character, an archetype popularised by Lord Byron. Byron himself was something of a legend in Branwell's time; he was considered one of the greatest poets, had involved himself in the Greek War of Independence, and had been embroiled in a number of romantic scandals, even facing accusations of a sexual relationship with his own half-sister, Augusta Leigh.

Byron's characters were just as large as life. Equipped with quick tempers, unparalleled skills, and deep wells of emotion, they dominated the page. Many heroes react to events or the actions of an antagonist, whereas Byronic characters are often the ones making things happen.

So when you read 'and the weary are at rest', you'll read about an Alexander Percy who has a temper that is 'short and sudden'; he is 'the best gun between Derbyshire and Westmoreland'; and his feelings have a 'wider higher and deeper range'. He is well-travelled, well-respected, and handsome. He fosters rebellion and disrespects the church. He's a troublemaker through and through; he was usually involved in any upheaval in Angria. If there is any doubt that both Byron and his characters were the model for Percy, it should be erased by the fact that Percy's wife was named Augusta; the same name as Byron's half-sister.

But although Percy would have been fun to write, I think Branwell's infatuation with the character went beyond the page. I believe Branwell wanted to *be* Alexander Percy.

Humble Origins

Why would Branwell model himself on his own Byronic character? Why not simply be Branwell Brontë? You have to remember that the Romantic poets were heroes and idols to the Brontës, and likely seemed more exciting than their own lives. Wordsworth was well travelled. Coleridge was largely responsible for the glamorised idea of a writer inspired by drug-fuelled dreams. And Byron's exploits excited and scandalised in equal measure; everyone likes a bad boy.

Despite his best efforts, Branwell lacked the means to study in London or travel the continent, nor could he indulge in drug-fuelled dreams when he lived in a parsonage or had to work for his coin. His only course would be to write, and be known for his words alone.

But that doesn't seem to have been enough. Branwell was almost breathless with 'a hope of entrance into the open world'[1] when he wrote to *Blackwood's Magazine* and to Wordsworth. This alone isn't remarkable, but a line written to Grundy of 'an ancient parsonage, among lonely hills which probably will never hear the whistle of an Engine till yourself and I are in the grave'[2] raises a question: was

Branwell trying to escape Haworth because he was embarrassed by it?

There is certainly a sense that Branwell was worried about what people thought of him; why else would he brag of imagined exploits and traits in letters to men who were not only meant to be his friends, but knew better than to believe them? Why would he write to John Brown, a man who knew him well, saying

> as to the young ones! – I have one sitting by me just now – fair-faced, blue eyes, dark haired sweet eighteen – she little thinks the devil is so near her![3]

And why would he claim to indulge in 'malignant yet cold debauchery'[4], describe himself as possessing 'unconquerable health'[5] and, even as he was approaching death, claim that he possessed 'a constitution still so strong that it will keep me years in torture and despair'[6]? No-one who knew him was likely to believe such claims. Who was Branwell trying to convince?

If he felt insecure enough to brag and lie to his friends, how must Branwell have felt about the rest of the world? Perhaps he feared the reaction when his work was identified as belonging to nothing more than a parson's son who had barely left provincial little Haworth?

But if he published under another name, a name that created mystery and intrigue, he could build up a body of work only to reveal himself at a later date. Perhaps when he had found the means to enter the world. Perhaps when he had accomplished enough to be worthy of the world's attention. Why not publish his poems under a pseudonym? Why not publish as Alexander Percy, Earl of Northangerland?

The Byron of Haworth

There is only one reason for a writer to use a pseudonym: to hide your identity from readers. Branwell's sisters, and plenty of other women of the time, did this so their work might be judged by its merits, rather than by their gender. Writers sometimes use a pseudonym to write in a new genre, without the baggage of previous work. Others use it because they want to separate their writing from their "real" life.

Branwell didn't face any of these problems when he wrote under the name "Northangerland". His reason for doing so can be gleaned from the choice of name itself. After all, it could not be as simple as merely liking it. Eventually Branwell would reveal himself as Northangerland and people would ask questions; the name would have to be explained. And Branwell would either have to invent an entirely new story or, more likely, he planned to tell them the truth. People would then compare Branwell with Percy, creator and created. Unless Branwell was determined to be found less exciting than his creation, it makes sense that he expected to come out favourably in the comparison. He expected to be found just as exciting, albeit perhaps less villainous, than Alexander Percy, Earl of Northangerland.

This perhaps explains why Branwell was always exaggerating his exploits; in the years to come, his friends and acquaintances would tell stories of a man who drank, seduced, and then wrote of life's experiences in a blaze of inspiration. Of a man whose creations were a reflection of himself.

I suspect this is what was going through his mind when he first noticed Lydia Robinson's interest. This would be an exploit worthy of a Byronic character. Don Juan had seduced married women. So had Alexander Percy. If Branwell could pull off the same feat, he would be one step closer to becoming Northangerland in truth.

And, of course, Lydia Robinson represented an escape from the drudgery of work; he admitted to Leyland that, as Robinson's husband, he expected to be wealthy. Better yet, wealth obtained by being a young, virile scoundrel capable of seducing a married woman.

But did Branwell seduce Lydia Robinson? Or was it just another exaggeration to impress his friends?

Was there an affair?

When Mr Robinson died in May 1846, it seemed there was nothing to stand between Branwell and his love (and his life of leisure). But there was no reunion. Instead there was a story that Mr Robinson had amended his will to keep them apart forever.

Charlotte explained to Ellen Nussey that:

> Mr Robinson had altered his will before he died and effectually prevented all chance of a marriage between his widow and Branwell by stipulating that she should not have a shilling if she ever ventured to reopen any communication with him[7]

Mr Robinson did alter his will shortly before he died, but to cut out one of his daughters; she had eloped with an actor he did not approve of, and so he disinherited her. There was no mention of Branwell, no restriction on who his widow could or could not marry. It was all a lie.

Someone in this story is not being honest. Either Lydia Robinson is lying to Branwell, or Branwell has invented a fantastical story to explain his dismissal from Thorp Green.

Lydia Robinson didn't do herself any favours when it came to her reputation, and for this reason she is usually credited as the source of the lie. Although Branwell told his friends that Lydia was 'distracted to the verge of insanity'[8], that she was plagued by 'sorrows and agonies'[9], that she still bore an 'inextinguishable love'[10] for him, the truth was somewhat different.

Following the death of her husband, it appears that, if Lydia had any feelings for Branwell, she certainly had no intention of marrying him. Instead she turned her gaze to more appropriate suitors. Sir Edward Scott was a distant relative, a wealthy landowner, and second Baronet of Scott of Great Barr. Scott was already married, but that doesn't seem to have discouraged Lydia. She moved her family into Scott's home and apparently made an effective play for his affections, given that she married him just three months after his wife passed away.

Lydia also sent several sums of money to Branwell in the years following his dismissal, which has been interpreted as hush money and a tacit admission of guilt. Given what she was up to, it's easy to understand why she would want to keep Branwell at bay.

The final apparent nail in the coffin of Lydia Robinson's reputation came when Elizabeth Gaskell published her biography of Charlotte Brontë, relating the story of the affair and placing the blame for it on Lydia. Lydia made no attempt to disprove Gaskell's allegations, but instead sought a successful legal retraction on the basis there was a lack of evidence. That she didn't simply present evidence of her own is often taken as proof that Gaskell was on to something.

But, in the same way that Gaskell's assassination of Branwell's character has unfairly stuck, I believe that her opinion of Lydia Robinson has persisted too. If we turn to Lydia's daughters, we can see signs that things might be a little different than previously thought.

From the Mouths of Babes

The news of Lydia Robinson's second marriage came to the Brontë family via Elizabeth and Mary Robinson, two of Lydia's daughters and Anne's former pupils. They had begun to send Anne letters six months after their father's death.

But the letters are interesting for more than the news they delivered, because they made no mention of any relationship between their mother and Branwell.

When Branwell told his friends and family of Lydia's distress, he cited as his source two of her employees and a doctor who was close to the family. If Lydia was spinning tales of altered wills, sorrows and agonies, and inextinguishable love for Branwell, why didn't she make sure her daughters were singing from the same hymn sheet?

To my mind there are five possible explanations why Lydia;s daughters did not acknowledge the affair:

1. They wanted no part in the lies; but given that their eldest sister (also called Lydia) had been disinherited and cut out of the family, it seems unlikely that Elizabeth and Mary wouldn't be willing to toe the line.
2. Branwell's hopes were already dashed and there was no need to lie further; but there was always a chance that his hopes would be revived and, as their mother was not yet remarried when they reopened correspondence with Anne, he could still ruin her plans to marry Scott.
3. They were ignorant of any improper conduct because her mother had hidden it from them; unlikely, as Lydia would then run the risk that her daughters would deny the tales of bitter tears and distress and encourage Branwell to return to Thorp Green.
4. They were simply ignoring the situation; they wouldn't be the first to pretend an embarrassing incident didn't exist.
5. They were ignorant of any improper conduct because there had been none; which would mean that there was no affair, and it had all been invented by Branwell.

Only two of these explanations make sense. Either Elizabeth and Mary were ignoring the uncomfortable truth of what happened between Branwell and their mother, or there was no uncomfortable truth at all; there had been no affair between Branwell and Lydia Robinson.

Lydia the Innocent?

In the absence of any evidence, many commenters believe Lydia's reputation is enough to suggest that there was an affair. But her "bad" reputation is all a matter of interpretation.

For instance, her marriage to Edward Scott has been characterised as a calculated effort to ensnare a wealthy husband to finance her lifestyle. The timing of their marriage, so soon after his wife's death, feels pretty unseemly to us now. But it wasn't unusual for the

1840s, and Lydia was hardly the first woman to pursue a man for his station and his wealth. She had grown accustomed to a certain standard of living that couldn't be supported by the income she received from her dead husband's estate (or, incidentally, a Haworth tutor's income). Perhaps her choice of husband and her method of securing him were calculated, but she was not alone in committing that "crime".

But what about the "hush money"? Today, as in 1846, it doesn't always matter if something is true for it to damage a person's reputation. How many lives have been ruined by allegations that cannot be shaken even after they've been disproven? Lydia might simply have been concerned that Branwell's version of events could hurt her, and keeping him away from Thorp Green was the best way of making sure his story wasn't heard where it could hurt her prospects.

Finally, this explains why Lydia threatened Gaskell's publishers with legal action without proving her innocence. She had to defend her reputation, but it is nigh on impossible to disprove such "he said, she said" allegations (as Gaskell demonstrated when she was unable to produce her own evidence).

None of this precludes either an affair or that Lydia was the one telling lies. But it does reset ideas about her reputation, which helps us look at the facts objectively. And, equally, we need to clear up a few things about Branwell too.

Born Storyteller

We know that Branwell brags and exaggerates. I've laid out how his embarrassment at his origins, his skill for invention, and his need to create a Byronic myth around himself explained his behavior in this regard. But is it possible he created the story of the affair? That it was all invented to impress people?

We have no-one else's testimony that there was an affair except for Branwell's. Patrick Brontë would talk about a gardener in the employ of the Robinson's who corroborated the story but, while such a gardener did exist, there's no evidence that he was involved in the scandal; only Branwell's word involved him in the narrative.

And so we are left relying on Branwell for details of what happened, which are suitably dramatic and overwrought, reading like something from his Angrian tales. Lord Houghton's description of one of Branwell's letters to John Brown mentions that Branwell took brandy before breakfast in order to face 'the AGONY of the day'[11], and adds that Branwell sent Brown a lock of Lydia's hair along with a description of how it has often lain on his breast at night.

Yet, when he is dismissed from Thorp Green, he meekly leaves behind a woman he apparently adores. Why? He offers an explanation to Grundy:

> Had I strength to return and meet him the results would be serious to one or both, but providence has hitherto denied me the power for I have lain during nine long weeks utterly shattered in body and broken down with mental despair.[12]

This is nothing more than bravado mixed with excuses. An 1840s equivalent of "he'd be in trouble if I didn't have to be somewhere else". And Branwell certainly wasn't 'broken down'; in those nine weeks, he had summoned the strength to visit Liverpool with John Brown and, according to a letter to Leyland, begun work on a novel. Branwell's letter to Grundy reads more like an excuse as to why there'd been no struggle for Lydia's affections. In fact, Branwell would often tell people that Mr Robinson had threatened to shoot him if he returned to Thorp Green; a convenient reason not to return.

And when Mr Robinson died? The insistence Branwell had shown of the love and passion he and Lydia had enjoyed would surely mean they would reunite. Unless there was another insurmountable obstacle. Like a will that forbade them to seek each other out, and an executor who threatened to, again, shoot Branwell on sight.

Is it possible that Branwell invented the affair? He has past form of inventing tales of his devilish interactions with pretty young women. Why not an older, wealthier, married woman? And is it beyond the realms of possibility that this tale got away from him, necessitating more and more lies to explain away why reality didn't fit with his version of events?

It's possible, but not likely. Branwell was an exaggerator, yes, but not an outright liar. You only need to look at the poetry he wrote after his dismissal to see that he was genuine in his feelings. Poems like 'Penmaenmawr' clearly have roots in the affair at Thorp Green, and he wrote a number of poems to Lydia as well.

The Middle Way

It seems to me that we have taken for granted that there was an affair purely because Branwell said so. But, as demonstrated, we cannot take him at his word. Once again, we need to ignore the "accepted wisdom" and decide for ourselves.

I suggest that there was something less than an affair. I suspect that Lydia Robinson was flirtatious with Branwell, encouraging him to imagine a *Don Juan*-like adventure for himself that would give him a reputation deserving of his pseudonym. His letter to John Brown feels authentic in its uncertainty when he asks his friend's opinion as to whether 'it is worth-while for him to go on to extremities'[13] with his employer's wife.

And I'm certain that Branwell and Lydia engaged in inappropriate behaviour, and maybe even crossed the line at times. But ultimately it was nothing more than occasional indiscretion. Lydia likely enjoyed the attentions of a younger man, and Branwell, encouraged by the Byronic fantasies of his youth and his desire to be more exciting than he really was, imagined something more for the future.

Such behaviour was certainly enough for Mr Robinson to dismiss Branwell, but this was not enough to concern Lydia. There was no future with Branwell; she wasn't about to impoverish herself to be with him. Yet she saw that his impassioned desire, so flattering when she could keep a lid on him, could be a problem; his interpretation of their relationship could damage her reputation.

But he could hurt her with spurned vengeance as much as with ardent desire, so she couldn't simply end any and all correspondence. As she couldn't visit or write to him directly without fanning the flames of gossip, she sent servants with money to keep him well disposed towards her.

She likely did lie to him. Perhaps she claimed to miss him. Branwell's ego (and the tales he had already told) translated that into devastation at their separation, and added excuses and threats against his life to explain why he didn't go back to Thorp Green.

And when Mr Robinson died, Lydia might have explained to Branwell that Robinson's will would stop the income from his estate when she remarried (which was standard practice for the time) and point out that Branwell didn't have the means to support her and her family.

But this would be an embarrassing ending to Branwell's Byronic adventure, so he exaggerated the will, claiming it forbade them from being together.

This, of course, is all conjecture, but I believe it fits the facts better than any other interpretation. It explains why only Branwell spoke of the affair (because Lydia didn't think there was one). It explains why Elizabeth and Mary seemed ignorant of it (because there wasn't much to know). It explains why Branwell acted as if there had been an affair (because he had allowed himself to imagine more between him and Lydia than there was). It explains why there was no evidence to contradict Gaskell's claims (because nothing much happened), but also explains why Lydia would want such allegations silenced (because enough happened to be scandalous). And it explains why she sent Branwell money (to keep him sweet and keep his version of events to himself).

After the Fact

The curse of Alexander Percy didn't end when Branwell was dismissed from Thorp Green. I've already mentioned the hardy constitution of a Byronic hero, as well as the bawdy Byronic drinking scenes the Brontës grew up reading. And those deep emotions of the Byronic hero, as well as the influence of figures like Coleridge and de Quincey, meant Branwell would imagine his great sorrows should be drowned in drink and drugs. He believed that he could handle it. That although he might look like Branwell Brontë, he was Northangerland within, and had the constitution to match. That whatever substances he threw at his body, they couldn't hurt him.

But, of course, Branwell wasn't Northangerland. He was exactly what he didn't want to be: a parson's son, neither more nor less exceptional than anyone else. What skill and talent he had with words was not matched with an iron constitution, nor was he immune to the addictions of drink and drugs.

Grundy claimed that it was Branwell's sorrows that killed him. He was wrong. It was Alexander Percy that killed Branwell Brontë. Or, at least, Branwell's worship of the Byronic ideal that Percy represented. Had Branwell not been trying to live up to his alter-ego, not been trying to earn his pseudonym, there would have been no affair, and no descent into drink, drugs, and addiction. Had Branwell been happy being Branwell, instead of trying to be someone else, he might have found the life in letters he dreamed of.

~

This chapter hasn't painted Branwell in the best light. But I promised I wasn't going to make him out to be a put-upon saint; he was as foolish as he was talented. But I think it's time to write about that talent. It's time to write about what made Branwell great: his poetry.

---

1. Letter 5
2. Letter 13
3. Letter 8
4. Letter 13
5. Letter 26
6. Letter 36
7. Juliet Barker, *The Brontës: A Life in Letters* (Viking, 1997) p. 148
8. Letter 30

9. Letter 30
10. Letter 32
11. Letter 21
12. Letter 26
13. Letter 20

BRANWELL BRONTË: THE POET

DON'T PANIC. YOU DON'T NEED TO "GET" POETRY TO READ THIS chapter. You won't need to know your iambic pentameter from your blank verse. We're just going to look at some of Branwell's poetry and try to use it to find out what made him tick.

We have to be wary of reading too much into Branwell's work. After all, invention is a writer's stock in trade. But even invention tells us a lot; someone who writes a lot about love, for example, clearly has something on their mind.

In Branwell's case, his poetry reveals that it was death he had on his mind, as well as what happened after death, and whether there was anyone behind it all. He used his poetry to try to work through these questions over his entire life. But the best place to start that journey is 1837.

Wordsworth's Ode

Branwell reached out to many established writers for approval, encouragement, and perhaps he hoped for patronage too. In 1837 it was William Wordsworth he appealed to, writing:

> I have ventured to come before one whose works I have most loved in our Literature and who most has been with me a divinity of the mind.[1]

He also included one of his poems, 'Still and bright in twilight gleaming'. It was not only an Angrian poem, but it was perhaps his most Wordsworthian; critics have pointed to the similarities it shares with Wordsworth's 'Ode: Intimations of Immortality'. It would be easy to say that he was trying to flatter the older poet with imitation. But Branwell was doing something much more complicated than that.

'Ode: Intimations of Immortality' suggests that, before our mortal lives on Earth, we have a heavenly existence that we can dimly remember when we are children. Our presence on Earth makes us forget this prior life.

Wordsworth describes this heavenly existence as a world 'Apparelled in celestial light'[2], and explains that 'Our souls have sight of that immortal sea...And see Children sport upon the shore'[3]. But our forgetfulness is an act of kindness; Earth has 'something of a Mother's mind'[4] and is a 'homely Nurse'[5] with 'no unworthy aim'[6]. Wordsworth sees the forgetfulness as an act of mercy, that the memory of a better existence doesn't pain us.

Branwell's Response

'Still and bright in twilight gleaming' explores the same idea of a prior heavenly existence, but with some key differences. Children remember this prior life, and it is due to Earth that we forget; 'Earth's shadow came 'tween it[the soul] and heaven'. Branwell continues the light-related imagery by explaining how the light of a newly-risen Moon transforms 'oaks so huge and hoary', which we can interpret as ourselves, aged and jaded, into more innocent 'fairy woodlands'. The light reminds us of the heavenly existence we've forgotten, just like Wordsworth's poem, and Branwell's work looks forward to a time when we will once again 'wake on that blest shore'.

A poor reflection

Both poems seem pretty similar, don't they? But already we can see a few differences. Earth has kindly blessed us with forgetfulness in Wordsworth's poem, whereas for Branwell it has rudely stepped between us and heaven. Wordsworth's poem is also almost a list of wonderful things in nature, rainbows and roses and moons and sunshine. Branwell's is full of 'tempests wild' and 'blighting floods of bitter tears'.

This is because Wordsworth accepts our exile from heaven, whereas Branwell does not. Wordsworth's poem ends with thankfulness, but Branwell's poem is one of blame. He sees us as 'from his hand perfected gone' until we are 'clothed in clay'; God makes us perfect, but by sending us to Earth, he sullies us. Furthermore, Earth is a place of temptation; Branwell fears 'the sons of earth / Will love the land that gave them birth' and that such a love will lead them 'through blood and flame, / From crime to crime' until 'All Hope of Heaven [is] for ever gone!'

Instead of mere imitation, Branwell was trying to show off to Wordsworth by inhabiting the older poet's original work and turning it on its head. Instead of accepting an exile from heaven, he questions it. He makes it plain that someone has deliberately cast us out and, worse, cast us into a place that puts our return in peril.

Milton

Although Branwell blamed God for our exile to Earth in 'Still and bright', he didn't explore the questions or consequences of that blame in the poem. It was enough to simply challenge Wordsworth. But he did return to the idea in 'Azrael: On the Eve of Destruction', in which an angel rises up in revolt against God.

Don't be surprised if that idea sounds familiar; the story of Satan's revolution and subsequent fall was familiar to the Brontë children too from John Milton's *Paradise Lost*. Published in 1667, it wasn't the first attempt to tell the story of the Fall, but it was the first popular telling in which Satan was viewed as anything other than evil. In fact, Satan is arguably the hero of *Paradise Lost*, and many Romantic readers would have read it the same way.

Whether it was Milton or Wordsworth who inspired God's villainous side when Branwell wrote 'Still and bright' at the age of 20, it was definitely Milton who inspired 'Azrael'.

Paradise Lost

Paradise Lost is the reason we have a modern romantic, hero version of Satan/Lucifer that we can empathise with and even root for.

> Not free, what proof could they have giv'n sincere
> Of true allegiance, constant Faith or Love,
> Where only what they needs must do, appear'd,
> Not what they would?
> ...
> What pleasure I from such obedience paid?[7]

Satan sees, if not evil in God's rule, then a certain mismanagement. Milton turns Satan into a character seeking to break the shackles God has imposed on us, and allow everyone to do as they will, whether or not that includes loyalty to their ruler.

> The strife which thou call'st evil, but wee style
> The strife of Glory: which we mean to win,
> Or turn this Heav'n into the Hell
> thou fablest, here however to dwell free,
> If not to reign[8]

Satan wants personal glory, and is so proud he would rather be free in Hell if he cannot reign in Heaven. He's willing to destroy what is good if he cannot have it for himself.

The Byronic heroes with which the Brontës were so taken had their beginnings in Milton's Satan. Rebellious, arrogant, and charming, Satan ostensibly declares his revolution in the name of freedom, but seeks power and glory for himself.

Azrael

Much like the relationship between 'Still and bright' and Wordsworth, Branwell's poem seems similar to Paradise Lost on the surface. Azrael, the angel of death (although he is not described as such in the poem), seeks to rise up in revolution. He, too, claims to be seeking liberty. But whereas Satan sought liberty from a tyrannical God, it isn't always clear what kind of liberty Azrael wants.

The poem begins with Noah standing over his father's grave, issuing a warning of the impending Flood. Noah is given 48 lines to state his case for 'God's just vengeance', but it is dismissed by Azrael as merely an attempt to 'embitter human joys'. Azrael also levels against God the same charge seen in 'Still and bright': that though God 'bids us turn from sin / He hedges us, with tempters, in'. Azrael demands liberty, and leads the crowd away from Noah and his warnings.

So far, so simple. But the second section of the poem sees Azrael admit a shocking belief: 'There is no God – I know there's none!' This raises a new question: is Azrael leading a rebellion against Christianity itself? Is Azrael, and by extension Branwell, declaring himself an atheist?

'Tis Man makes God

Branwell has often been labelled an atheist. Collins called him a 'purposeful atheist'[9], whilst Gerin claimed that he 'not only refused to go to his father's church and join in the family prayers, but had openly attacked such practices as pure hypocrisy'[10]. But if Branwell was an atheist, he was a silent one; to be an atheist was an uncommon (and unpopular) thing. It hadn't been so long ago that Percy Shelley had been temporarily expelled from university for writing an essay called 'The Necessity of Atheism'.

So we would likely know if Branwell had openly declared himself an atheist, especially given he was the son of a priest. Even if the family had tried to hide it, it is hard to believe there wouldn't be some sort of evidence. Unless, of course, the evidence is his poetry.

'Azrael' seems like a prime example of such evidence. Azrael himself bids his audience to banish 'phantasies! – / Just trust your reason and your eyes!', and points out that 'We say this world was made by One / Who's seen or heard or known by none'. And then, of course, says to himself that 'There is no God – I know there's none!'

Azrael is alone when he makes this bold claim, which could be read as Branwell allowing himself a private admission on the page. Or it could simply be a narrative device, a character trying to persuade himself that Noah was wrong and that there is nothing to fear in rebellion.

The claim is complicated by the introduction of the character Marah. Marah features in the Bible as a place where the water is too bitter to drink. The name is also similar to that of Maria, Branwell's older sister who died when he was seven. We'll come back to Maria later.

For now, Marah is fatally ill; she must 'descend to clay'. But she struggles from her deathbed to refute Azrael's denials of God; she has seen Him in a dream. Marah tells Azrael of a 'voice divine', of 'Heaven's unutterable shine', and even confirms Noah's warnings that 'Over this heedless Earth they'll spread a shoreless main!'

Damnation

Marah's waters, or at least her dreams, are indeed too bitter for Azrael; he dismisses her warnings as the ravings of an ill woman. But he is presented with a 'strange night of utter gloom, / Those gathering clouds, that boding sky / That mournful wind bewailing by'; empirical evidence of the storm Noah warned of.

But Azrael continues to deny God, and is visited by Moloch. Branwell likely borrowed Moloch from Milton and, while Branwell calls him a 'tempter', in *Paradise Lost* Moloch claims 'Of wiles, / More unexpert, I boast not'[11]. He certainly doesn't work hard to persuade Azrael to fall and, once Azrael drinks from his tempter's goblet, the dreams of liberty are gone, and the two plot an insurrection together, deciding amongst themselves 'who should 'scape and who should fall'.

'Azrael' seems to suggest, then, that there is a God. Noah's warns of the Flood, and Marah's dream and the evidence seen by Azrael's own eyes support those warnings. When Azrael denies this evidence, he falls from noble freedom fighter to base insurrectionist. If Branwell was an atheist, why would he debase Azrael and undermine his claim that there is no God?

There is a school of thought that suggests Branwell didn't reject Heaven, but that he felt it rejected him. Some, such as Gerin, have argued that Aunt Branwell's strict Calvinistic beliefs, which focused heavily on sin and damnation, led Branwell to believe he was too much a sinner for Heaven.

Although this theory relies on casting Aunt Branwell as a harsh, stern, and unloving indoctrinator (which, as I have already explained, is incorrect), there is an element that rings true: Branwell's sense of sin.

The perils of pleasure

The key to God's guilt in 'Still and bright', as well as 'Azrael', were the Earthly pleasures and the tempters He surrounds us with, which threaten our return to Heaven. Branwell would often ruminate on the dangers of pleasure, and 'Black Comb' is perhaps his best exploration of the idea. Named after the mountain he saw whilst working for Robert Postlethwaite in Broughton, Branwell describes Black Comb as 'half revealed, 'mid shade and light' and 'half smiles, half frowns'. If Black Comb seems only half-happy, that might be an overstatement. The poem goes on to explain that Black Comb would rather 'fight / A thousand years of struggles with a storm / Than bask one hour subdued by sunshine warm'.

Why endure such a harsh existence? Because Black Comb knows

that too much happiness is a weakness; by spending so much time in struggle, the mountain is 'invincible'. Meanwhile, 'Man loses vigour in unstable joys'.

Branwell deliberately separates this last line from the others by form. It is begun and ended in a single line, and it stands outside the rhyme scheme, jarring the reader in order to make its point. This line is the crux of the poem; Branwell is concerned that pleasure is weakening him.

The comfort of pleasure

Branwell's concerns over pleasure appear to continue into his employment on the railways. An unpublished poem titled only 'Dec/19 1841 at Luddenden Church' begins with a lament that he is enmeshed in 'pleasure's wiles' and, once again, he turns to the hope of a 'stern sustaining power'.

But this poem's lament is explicitly directed to God and, in the final few lines, Branwell explains why he needs such strength: to 'look into the past, / And see that darkly shadowed hour / Which I must meet at last'.

So Branwell needs strength to face the hour he must meet, i.e. death. And he recognises that pleasures won't give him that strength. But, most interestingly, Branwell needs to look into the past to face death. Why? Because of the death he has already witnessed.

Maria

Branwell was just seven when his older sister, Maria, died, and we don't need to imagine that this death had a traumatic impact on him. All of his writing, from juvenilia to poetry to prose, is filled with characters called Maria, Mary, Marah, and more variants. So many of them are figures of beauty and perfection, and so many of them die.

Remember Marah, from 'Azrael', who had a beatific vision of God and was fated to die? She is joined by Mary Percy, daughter of Alexander Percy from the Angrian tales and whom Branwell killed twice. Standing alongside them is Maria Thurston, the love interest of Alexander Percy in Branwell's attempt at a novel. And there is another Mary in the last of Branwell's published poems, appropriately titled *The End of All.* Once again, Mary is dying. But Branwell is more explicit about his relationship with Maria, death, and God, in this poem than in any other.

Heaven denied

Mary's husband, the narrator of the poem, describes how 'Sweet holy words to me she said, / Of that bright heaven which shone so near', but that 'soon enough, all words were over' and that '*mine* was not her heavenward eye'; he sees only a 'starless waste'. Where Mary sees a heavenly afterlife, he does not.

Does he fail to see it because it is hidden from him, or because it isn't there? Does he fear he cannot be as good and worthy as Maria, or does he fear that heaven is, to use Azrael's words, a fantasy?

If we look at *Peaceful Death and Painful Life*, it seems to suggest a lack of faith; Branwell describes the 'happy dead' as lying in an 'earthly bed', where they 'sleep...dreamless'. There is no God here, no afterlife. The dead lie where we leave them, peaceful but inert.

But if we look at an unpublished poem Branwell wrote in Mary Pearson's Commonplace Book, we can find a line reading 'Life's rough road / May end, at last, in rest with GOD.'

Was Branwell an Atheist?

As with so many things, the truth lies between extremes. It isn't as simple as labeling Branwell an atheist or a believer; it's more complicated than that. All of the Brontë sisters had a crisis of faith in their lives, and it is clear that Branwell was no exception. But where his sisters managed to find their faith again, I suspect Branwell *wanted* to be an atheist. When you read Azrael's quiet, solitary defiance of the existence of God, or a husband left with no heavenward eye after his wife dies, or the dead described as sleeping and inert, it doesn't tally with a belief in God.

Why, then, write such lines as 'Life's rough road / May end, at last, in rest with GOD'? Or have empirical evidence and divine visions undermine Azrael's atheism?

Just as Maria's death had an impact on Branwell, so did her life. He heard her 'sweet holy words' when he was young and impressionable. Maria represented a perfect, devout vision of Christianity for her younger siblings; Charlotte described her 'prematurely developed and remarkable intellect, as well as the mildness, wisdom, and fortitude of her character'[12]. And, as Helen Burns in *Jane Eyre*, Maria portrayed 'eternity a rest – a mighty home – not a terror and an abyss'[13].

And yet, despite her fervent faith, Maria had been taken from the family, taken young and by a hideous illness. The loss of a loved one has, is, and always will be a source of religious doubt, and Branwell was no exception. The idea that he wanted to abandon the faith that had taken Maria, a faith he felt had abandoned him, perfectly fits the conflicting portrayal of God and death in his poetry. He couldn't shake the teachings he had been given by Maria and so, at each turn, he steps back from stepping into atheism. Branwell left himself hovering at the edge of his own rebellion against God, and in perpetual doubt over what would happen when he died.

If Branwell's poetry can shed light on his faith, perhaps it can shed light on a hotly-contested question: did he sire an illegitimate child whilst working for Robert Postlethwaite?

Was Branwell a Father?

'Letter From a Father on Earth to His Child in Her Grave' is the source of the question, ad I outlined how little evidence there is to answer it, so our only hope of an answer is the poem itself. At first glance, it's easy to see why readers assumed Branwell had been a father. Aside from the title, the poet is explicitly writing to his dead child, mourning the loss of 'the twilight star of childhood', and appears to see through a subterfuge of 'springtide flowers' to 'winters withered grass beneath'. And while others might recoil from the child's corpse now, the poet only remembers 'beauty, innocence, and smiles'.

But any child would have been born after Branwell had been sent back to Haworth. There is no evidence that Branwell ever returned to Broughton-in-Furness, so these smiles can only be imagined.

Imagination is a problem for anyone using this poem to prove Branwell's fatherhood; it's a writer's prerogative to invent. Could this simply be an invented father, the dead child a literary device?

More of the same

A closer reading of the poem reveals that is less about the child and more about the father. A father whose heart many 'think a worthless stone'. A father who envies a daughter who no longer 'feels distraction's throb nor pleasure's thrill'. A father 'hopelessly gazing – ever hesitating/'Twixt miseries'. A father plagued by 'troubled pleasures soon chastised by fear' (a line echoed in a letter Branwell wrote to Francis Grundy) and able to lift 'a voice of joy that THOU art freed from care'.

It all sounds rather familiar, doesn't it? Branwell's troubled relationship with pleasure, his dour sense of misery and care, and ideas that the dead sleep dreamless and untroubled. It doesn't feel like Branwell is mourning the death of a real child. Instead it feels that he is using an idea of a child to explore his favourite themes, just as he used the idea of a corpse in 'Real Rest', and the idea of a dying wife in 'End of All'.

Does this rule out the possibility that Branwell was a father? No. It's possible that he wrote this poem to a real child but that he was too wrapped up in himself to stay on topic. But I don't think this is likely. The poem was published in April 1846, at a time when he was writing poetry and a novel, and boasting to Leyland of sending 'materials for a respectably sized volume'[14] to a London publisher. He had not yet shrunk into the selfish despair that would tarnish the last years of his life, and I don't think he was yet self-absorbed enough to write about himself so much if he was truly mourning the death of his daughter.

Even if you disagree, the fact that the poem reads and feels too much like Branwell's other poems, which were not autobiographical, just throws too much doubt on the question of his fatherhood. Considering the poem was the source of the question, you would expect something more convincing. As it is, it feels like a sniff of an idea that has started a hunt for facts to support it.

The absence of those facts only highlights how little weight this poem lends to the idea of Branwell's fatherhood. It doesn't really suggest he was a father, and facts that don't really suggest it either.

I think it's time to close the lid on the matter; Branwell wasn't a father.

Of course, the Brontës are known for more than poetry. Charlotte, Emily, and Anne are perhaps better known for their novels, and we know that Branwell was writing one too. After his death, the testimony of some of his friends raised an ugly idea that Branwell's novel actually saw publication, but under Emily's name. It's an idea that has been dismissed, ridiculed, and hotly contested by a few. But is there any truth to it? Was Branwell the true author of *Wuthering Heights*?

---

1. Letter 6
2. William Wordsworth, *Wordsworth: Poetical Works*, ed. Thomas Hutchinson, revised Ernest De Selincourt, (Oxford University Press, 1969) p. 460, l.4
3. William Wordsworth, *Wordsworth: Poetical Works*, ed. Thomas Hutchinson, revised Ernest De Selincourt, (Oxford University Press, 1969) p. 461, l.167...170
4. William Wordsworth, *Wordsworth: Poetical Works*, ed. Thomas Hutchinson, revised Ernest De Selincourt, (Oxford University Press, 1969) p. 460, l.79
5. William Wordsworth, *Wordsworth: Poetical Works*, ed. Thomas Hutchinson, revised Ernest De Selincourt, (Oxford University Press, 1969) p. 460, l.81
6. William Wordsworth, *Wordsworth: Poetical Works*, ed. Thomas Hutchinson, revised Ernest De Selincourt, (Oxford University Press, 1969) p. 460, l.80

7. John Milton, *Paradise Lost*, Book III, (Oxford World's Classics, 2008) p. 64-65, l. 103-107
8. John Milton, *Paradise Lost*, Book VI, (Oxford World's Classics, 2008) p. 150, l. 289-293
9. Branwell Brontë, *The Hand of the Arch-Sinner*, edited by Robert Collins (Clarendon Press, 1993) p. xxxi
10. Winnifred Gerin, *Branwell Brontë: A Biography* (Hutchinson & Co, 1972) p. 294
11. John Milton, *Paradise Lost*, Book II, (Oxford World's Classics, 2008) p. 31, l. 51-52
12. Juliet Barker, *The Brontës: A Life in Letters* (Viking, 1997) p. 9
13. Charlotte Brontë, *Jane Eyre*, (Penguin Popular Classics, 1994) p.61
14. Letter 28

DID BRANWELL WRITE WUTHERING HEIGHTS?

When the Brontë sisters first published *Poems*, it was under the pseudonyms of Currer, Ellis, and Acton Bell (Charlotte, Emily, and Anne respectively). It was Emily and Anne who insisted on the protection of their privacy, but Charlotte also saw the benefits of concealing their gender: 'we had a vague impression that authoresses are liable to be looked on with prejudice'[1]. Charlotte wasn't wrong on this point. No secret lasts forever and, when the truth finally came out, there was a degree of shock and mutterings of indecency that weren't limited to the critics. Charlotte herself wrote:

> Whether it is right or advisable to create beings like Heathcliff, I do not know: I scarcely think it is.[2]

When Charlotte added her first foreword to *Wuthering Heights*, after Emily's death, she added something of an apology, explaining that Emily wrote such a savage and brutal work because she was shy and retiring; she learnt of people through hearsay and gossip, and thus heard the worst of them. Not knowing any better, this ugly face of humanity was the one she portrayed.

This idea of Emily as innocent to the point of ignorance is patronising, incorrect, and belittles both Emily and her work. But it was an idea that was already gathering steam. How could a woman write something as dark and terrible as *Wuthering Heights*?

Perhaps the question would have gone away if it weren't for Branwell's friends.

The *Halifax Guardian*, which had printed many of Branwell's poems, published in 1867 an extract of an article that expressed astonishment that *Wuthering Heights* could have been written by a woman. The paper received a letter in response from William Dearden, schoolmaster of Keighley, Huddersfield and Bradford. Dearden was a poet in his own right and a friend of Branwell's, and related in his letter the following story:

> Many years ago Patrick Brontë and I agreed that each should write a drama or a poem the principal character in which was to have a real or imaginary existence before the Deluge; and that, in a month's time, we should meet at the Cross Roads Inn, which is about half way between Keighley and Haworth, and produce the results of our lucubrations. We met at the time and place appointed, and in the presence of a mutual friend, the late J. B. Leyland, the promising sculptor. I read the first act of "The Demon Queen"; but when Branwell dived into his hat, the usual receptacle of his fugitive scraps, where he supposed he had deposited his M.S. poem, he found he had by mistake placed there a number of stray leaves of a novel on which he had been trying his 'prentice hand. Chagrined at the disappointment he had caused, he was about to return the papers to his hat, when both friends earnestly pressed him to read them, as they felt a curiosity to see how he could wield the pen of a novelist. After some hesitation he complied with the request, and riveted our attention for about an hour, dropping each sheet, when read, into his hat. The story broke off abruptly in the middle of a sentence, and he gave us the sequel *viva voce*, together with the real names of the prototypes of his characters; but, as some of these personages are still living, I refrain from pointing them out to the public. He said he had not yet fixed upon a title for his production, and was afraid he

> should never be able to meet with a publisher who would have the hardihood to usher it into the world. The scene of the fragment which Branwell read, and the characters introduced into it – so far as then developed – were the same as those in "Wuthering Heights", which Charlotte Brontë confidently asserts was the production of her sister Emily.[3]

It's a bold claim, and one that found an ally in Edward Sloane, another friend of Branwell's from Halifax, who also claimed that Branwell had read *Wuthering Heights* to him chapter by chapter as it was written.

Finally, Francis Grundy, Branwell's friend from the railways, also maintained that 'Patrick [Branwell] Brontë declared to me, and what his sister said bore out the assertion, that he wrote a great portion of *Wuthering Heights* himself. Indeed, it is impossible for me to read that story without meeting with many passages which I feel certain *must* have come from his pen.'[4]

Three men, well-acquainted with Branwell, claimed that he was the true author of *Wuthering Heights*. Is it possible that they are right, and that *Wuthering Heights* is the subject of a literary cover-up that has lasted 150 years?

No.

Three friends, three problems

I can guess that you're in one of two camps right now. You're either nodding along and thinking "quite right", or you're aghast and thinking how I could so categorically dismiss the possibility.

Of course it is impossible to be absolutely certain, with no shadow of a doubt, that the manuscript wasn't written by Branwell's hand and passed off as Emily's. But I can be certain enough, because there are three problems with the claim: Branwell's friends, Emily, and Branwell himself.

The Pal Problem

The first thing to do is clear up the issue of the claimants. First we can quickly dismiss the claims of Edward Sloane for one simple reason: he never made them publicly. We have only Dearden's word that Sloane agreed with him, which amounts to nothing more than "don't believe me? Well my friend thinks so too". That leaves Dearden's and Grundy's claims to deal with.

Perhaps the biggest problem with these claims is the date they were made. Dearden's was the first, and it didn't appear until 1867, almost twenty years after Branwell's death and the publication of *Wuthering Heights*. How well do you remember a meeting from twenty years ago? Or, better, how well do you remember a book you read twenty years ago? If I now gave you a book under a different name, could you be certain if it was the same one you read twenty years ago?

I'd be amazed if you could. We should also bear in mind that, as a friend of the Brontë family, there is little chance that Dearden didn't read the novel as soon as he learnt it was written by Emily. Yet he didn't make these claims when he first read it. Why not?

I suspect that Dearden read Gaskell's biography of Charlotte and, in defending the Brontë family against her cruel claims, he might have remembered that Branwell was writing a novel. He might even have remembered some of the details and, after reading that article in The *Halifax Guardian*, he put two and two together and unfortunately came up with five.

If Dearden's was the only claim, that might put the matter to bed. But what about Grundy?

People I Knew

Francis Grundy's own claim also came many years later, and is therefore suspect for the same reasons. But, unlike Dearden, Grundy's motives seem to have been rather less heroic. Rather than defending Branwell's honour, Grundy was trying to make himself look good.

Grundy wrote extensively about Branwell in his book *Pictures of the Past: Memories of Men I have Met and Places I have Seen*. The book was an autobiography and, without belittling it, there is an element of boasting in those pages. Grundy drops names and places to impress, and Branwell was no exception:

> I made the acquaintance of a genius of the highest order, Patrick Branwell Brontë, who was at least as talented as any member of that wonderful family. Much my senior, Brontë took an unusual fancy to me, and I continued, perhaps, his most confidential friend through good and ill until his death.[5]

These words are carefully phrased to flatter Grundy himself more than Branwell. According to Grundy, Branwell is a genius, but Grundy was able to snare his fancy and confidence, suggesting to the reader that Grundy must be terribly interesting.

Such is the flavour of Grundy's testimony, and so it cannot be trusted. He called Luddenden Foot station 'a rude wooden hut, with no village at hand', and claimed that they suffered from 'few books, little to do, no prospects, and wretched pay'[6]; all claims that are demonstrably untrue.

The question is whether Grundy suffered from a poor memory, or if he deliberately repeated Dearden's claims to make Branwell, and by extension himself, a more interesting character. Whatever your opinion might be, the result is the same: we can't trust Grundy's testimony either.

Emily the Innocent

Perhaps it is fitting that the best example of the argument against Emily having written *Wuthering Heights* comes from Grundy:

> It is well-nigh incredible that a book so marvellous in its strength, and in its dissection of the most morbid passions of diseased minds, could have been written by a young girl like Emily Brontë, who

> never saw much of the world or knew much of mankind, and whose studies of life and character, if they are entirely her own, must have been chiefly evolved from her own imagination.[7]

It is certainly true that Emily spent most of her life in Haworth, and her detractors seize upon this fact to "prove" that she would have been incapable of creating such brutal characters. How, they ask, could she have conceived of such things, when all she had to draw on was a sheltered existence in a humble parsonage?

Of course, *Jane Eyre* and *Agnes Grey* were written in a humble parsonage. And Emily did not spend her entire life there. She too attended Cowan Bridge, the school that claimed the lives of Maria and Elizabeth and inspired Lowood in *Jane Eyre*. Emily lived through the same harsh existence Charlotte described in her novel.

She attended Roe Head too, worked as a teacher at Law Hill School in Halifax, and studied in Brussels with Charlotte. She may not have spent much time in the world, and she certainly preferred life in Haworth. But it just isn't possible to say she 'never saw much of the world or knew much of mankind'.

Emily the Writer

Grundy also arms Emily with the only tool she needed to create characters such as Heathcliff: her imagination. This is something I've already touched upon, but it bears repeating. Grundy, and so many of Emily's detractors, forget that a writer does not need to have seen or experienced a thing to write about it. They also forget that she consumed the same literature that her siblings did. Even if she had been somehow incapable of conceiving of a man like Heathcliff, the works of Lord Byron had already given her plenty of examples and templates.

It seems to me that Emily suffers somewhat from the same accusation that is often found in theories that Shakespeare didn't write his own plays: 'how could *they* have written *this*?' The answer to this question was summarised by Neil Gaiman when he wrote: 'I would have thought that all one needs to understand people is to be a person.'[8] Charlotte didn't need to witness a madwoman locked in an attic to write Bertha Rochester, Anne didn't need to have a son to write Helen Graham, and Emily didn't need to experience the tortured, violent love of *Wuthering Heights*. All Emily needed to be was Emily in order to create Heathcliff and his cohorts.

Emily the sister

The notion that Branwell wrote *Wuthering Heights* also raises a new question: why would he ask Emily to pass it off as her own?

Branwell had written to his friends about his novel, and he even sought their opinion on publication. Joseph Leyland's father had once owned The *Halifax Guardian*, and thus would likely have known enough contacts in the publishing industry for Branwell to exploit. Branwell had also suggested in a letter to Leyland the possibility of approaching Henry Moxon. It seems unlikely that Branwell, with published poetry to his name and a few contacts that might help, could not have at least put his novel in front of a publisher.

Alice Law has suggested that Branwell didn't want his name attached to *Wuthering Heights*, that he would 'naturally shrink from any open acknowledgement of having portrayed his unhappy infatuation for a woman well known in the county' (*Law*, p.178). She also suggests that Branwell's estrangement from Charlotte meant that he couldn't admit to having written a novel.

Instead it was presented as Emily's, and she couldn't admit to the true authorship once it was published as the reviews were not favourable, and would only confirm Charlotte's poor opinion of Branwell. Law paints Emily as a brave, silently-suffering shield for Branwell, but there is not a scrap of evidence to suggest this.

We already know that Branwell was ready to tell anyone and everyone about his relationship with Lydia Robinson, and the existence of the published poems 'Real Rest' and 'Penmaenmawr' both alluded to his feelings.

And Branwell was just as open and vocal about his novel, and likely inspired Charlotte to start writing her own; she was working on *The Professor* in April 1846, a mere seven months after Branwell's announcement.

We can only guess at the reasons he wasn't included into his sisters' quest for publication. But to suggest Branwell smuggled a novel into their venture under Emily's name dismisses Emily's talent. It also doesn't make any sense.

Besides, you only have to read *Wuthering Heights* to realise it wasn't written by Branwell.

The Percy Problem

Although Branwell was a published poet, he had written plenty of prose too; his juvenilia is full of it, and plenty of it was filled with his favourite character, Alexander Percy. And, just as he reworked Angrian poems for publication, so he turned to that old prose when he came to write a novel.

In December 1837 Branwell began a story involving Percy and Maria Thurston, a married woman who naturally is drawn to Percy simply because he is Percy. There is not much to the story and Branwell never finished it. But he did pick it up again in 1845 and began to work it into a longer narrative which is known today as 'and the weary are at rest'.

Of course, the fact that Branwell was writing a novel about Alexander Percy doesn't mean he couldn't have also written *Wuthering Heights* at the same time. It is physically possible that Branwell could have written a novel that didn't feature Percy and marked an incredible improvement in is prose-writing skills (because 'and the weary are at rest' is, frankly, not very good). But is it emotionally possible? No. Branwell was too involved in the source material of 'and the weary are at rest'; the departure from his self and his obsessions in order to write *Wuthering Heights* would have been too drastic.

I am Heathcliff/Percy

To say that Branwell was preoccupied in 1845 is an understatement; his letters and his poems were filled with comments about his misery, his devotion to Lydia Robinson, his hopes that they would be reunited. His prose was no exception. It speaks volumes that, of all the tales he had written in his younger years about Alexander Percy, Branwell picked the one about Percy and a married woman to rework into his novel.

Whether or not you agreed with me that the affair was not as real as Branwell liked to make out, it's undeniable that Branwell's new muse of forlorn, thwarted love wasn't going anywhere.

'and the weary are at rest' acts as a form of wish-fulfillment for Branwell. Whereas, in reality, Lydia Robinson didn't fall at Branwell's feet, Maria Thurston falls for Percy's charms because, well, how could she not? This is Branwell's *Don Juan*, so the married woman is defenceless against the hero's charms. Maria Thurston's only refuge of resistance is her sense of duty. This would have been the perfect reason to give to Branwell as to why an affair couldn't progress, or perhaps Branwell invented it himself to explain why he was kept at a distance. Either way, a responsibility to marital duty is a convenient way of avoiding bruised egos and doesn't detract from anyone's charms; more wish-fulfillment.

If we were in any doubt that Branwell was obsessed with his Lydia-fantasy, we need only look at a poem he wrote in June 1846 titled 'Lydia Gisborne' (Gisborne being Lydia Robinson's maiden name). Although he wrote that his hopes were cast into 'woe's far deeper sea', more telling in the scribble in the margin: 'Lydia B–'. Like a lovesick teenager, Branwell was giving Lydia his surname; he simply could not let go of her.

What about Wuthering Heights?

Branwell was incapable of writing *Wuthering Heights*. Even if his talent could have risen enough to produce the novel, it contains nothing of interest to him; no Percy, no Lydia, no married women and affairs, no Byronic heroes (no, Heathcliff is not a hero).

But my opinion shouldn't be enough to convince you, and it doesn't have to be. The words written by Branwell and Emily are convincing enough.

Heroes

It isn't much of a surprise that Heathcliff shocked reader when *Wuthering Heights* was first published; he is often violent, he swears, he plots and uses people to exact revenge decades after a wrong, and he is often depicted as lacking basic human compassion.

At first glance, the Percy of 'and the weary are at rest' is much the same. Within the first few (existing) pages, he threatens each of his companions with violence, from knocking out teeth to sending them to 'Leeds infirmary to be tapped' (i.e. bled). But acts of violence are limited to giving his groom a shaking; he never actually hurts anyone. We can assume that he is capable of violence from the way other characters back down when he glares at them but, where Heathcliff lays hands on plenty of characters and dogs, Percy is all bark and no bite.

That's because Percy is a hero or, at least, Branwell's hero. He is meant to excite us with his dark tempers and his violent nature, but we are meant to root for him nonetheless. That's why other characters, and the narrator as well, heap such praise on him; Percy is the best shooter, possesses unmatched musical abilities, and is rich to boot. Even the interminable sequence where Percy tricks the Methodists into letting him and his gang offer hypocritical sermons is meant to awe the reader.

Heathcliff is not meant to evoke fond feelings. The other characters refer to him as a 'goblin'[9], a 'fiend'[10], and 'something other than a man'[11]. While it's possible to empathise with his desire for revenge on those who did him wrong, readers don't root for his success.

Finally, Heathcliff disappears for three years. When he leaves, he is uneducated and poor; when he returns, he is well-spoken and rich.

Nelly guesses that he might have been a soldier, but no details are ever given as to how Heathcliff came by his fortune. That doesn't seem to fit with the idea that Branwell could be the author; when he wrote about Percy, he spent pages alluding to, and then explicitly showing, his career as a pirate. Ignoring years of adventures just doesn't seem to fit Branwell's style.

Angria vs the Heights

Reading 'and the weary are at rest', you'll find it populated with Angrian characters. Alexander Percy, William and Maria Thurston, Quashia Quamina, Robert King (who was S'death), Hector Montmorency, and plenty more. When we looked at Branwell's poetry, we saw he had a habit of revisiting past work, polishing it and publishing it. He took the same approach with 'and the weary are at rest', resurrecting an old tale but relocating it to England. As late as 1845, Branwell was still mining the huge body of work that he and Charlotte had created as children.

Wuthering Heights contains no Angrian characters, and only one bears any resemblance: Joseph, the hectoring servant at the Heights, has a dialect and surly disposition similar to Robert King, or S'death, who was a feature of Branwell's juvenilia for so long that it's no surprise that Emily borrowed elements.

In fact, Juliet Barker points to Gondal for the origin of Heathcliff. Gondal was to Emily and Anne what Angria was to Charlotte and Branwell, and Barker claims that Heathcliff is a recreation of Gondal character Douglas, whose origins:

> were shrouded in mystery and who was doomed from birth to be blighted by fate; sadistic and cruel, Douglas' redeeming feature was his passionate love for the ambitious queen of Gondal.[12]

Of course, if Emily could borrow S'death, couldn't Branwell borrow Douglas? Not easily. Emily kept her work private; she was furious when Charlotte read her poetry, so it isn't likely that Branwell knew about Douglas.

But it's Emily's poetry that helps banish the idea of Angria from *Wuthering Heights*. Like Branwell, Emily hadn't abandoned her fantasy world, and she continued to write Gondal poetry even after she had published *Wuthering Heights*.

Poetry, both Emily's and Anne's, is all that remains of Gondal; the prose is lost, meaning the narrative is difficult to piece together. While some have tried to find stories and characters that foreshadow *Wuthering Heights*, this is mostly conjecture and hard to rely on. But the poetry itself gives us the heart of *Wuthering Heights*. Emily writes of a 'slighted heart'[13] and one character declares 'could I know thy soul with equal grief was torn –/This fate might be endured – this anguish might be borne!'[14], which calls to mind Heathcliff's reasons for leaving and the cruel passion he shares with Catherine.

And another poem refuses to hate the dead for their sins, asking

> Do I despise the timid deer
>   Because his limbs are fleet with fear?
>   Or would I mock the wolf's death-howl
>   Because his form is gaunt and foul?[15]

One of the key themes of *Wuthering* Heights is that a person's nature not only wins out over their surroundings, but that they should be loved despite a foul nature.

There are no such themes or thoughts in Branwell's Angrian work, but Emily's poetry shows just how much of Gondal there is in *Wuthering Heights*.

Romance

Wuthering Heights is often described as a romance, but it isn't until the end of the novel that a true romance is allowed to blossom. All other pairings are based on lies, deceit, and violence. Heathcliff lures Cathy into loving Linton, and their courtship is 'very pretty and very silly'[16];

Heathcliff lures Isabella into loving him, and immediately abandons his deception; Catherine lures Edgar into loving her, though she only regards him for his looks and his money. Other than Cathy and Hareton, the only honest love is between Heathcliff and Catherine, and even that is unromantic; Catherine's love for Heathcliff is almost crude, based not on admiration of his qualities, but 'because he's more myself than I am'[17]. And that love is discarded so that she can enjoy a better social station with Edgar.

'and the weary are at rest' contains a very different picture of romance. Percy desires Maria Thurston, the wife of his friend William Thurston. Percy doesn't seduce Maria; he doesn't have to. He only has to enter a room, declare he has no more interest in shooting that day, and Maria is at risk of a 'breach of promises given to her furious husband'. This is because Maria is a neglected wife, and Percy's love will save her from such neglect. It is simplistic, almost heroic, romance, and, as I have mentioned, wish-fulfillment based on Branwell's own romance with Lydia Robinson.

Heathcliff and Percy love in very different ways. Percy is all words; he rhapsodises over and over about how he would either protect or improve Maria. He repeatedly declares that 'every sinew would rouse to save your little finger from harm', or that he would 'exert my superior bodily strength save to preserve her from harm or my more impetuous temper save to infuse vigour into her mildness.' It is a very poetical seduction, and Maria is left 'powerless under the impulse of contenting feelings'.

Heathcliff declares his feelings only through a filter of anger and anguish. 'I love *my* murderer', he says, referring to Catherine, and then asks her 'would *you* like to live with your soul in the grave?'[18] But there are no tender scenes between them, no sweet words. Heathcliff loves, violently and with no tenderness. Percy loves with nothing but tenderness.

Death

Branwell had a complicated relationship with death, one I explored through his poetry in the previous chapter. But the ideas about death in *Wuthering* Heights are incompatible with those in Branwell's poetry.

The death of his older sister, Maria, had a very clear impact on Branwell. Death troubled him throughout his life, and he wrote about death as a release from the cares and troubles of life, not because there was an eternal and blissful hereafter, but because the dead could rest as dreamless sleepers. But *Wuthering Height*'s Nelly Dean tells Lockwood:

> I am seldom otherwise than happy while watching in the chamber of death...I see a repose that neither earth nor hell can break, and I feel an assurance of the endless and shadowless hereafter – the Eternity they have entered – where life is boundless in its duration, and love in its sympathy, and joy in its fullness.[19]

A viewpoint at odds with Branwell's, but which could easily be ascribed to Emily, who was arguably too young to be drastically affected by the loss of her older sisters. But this is not the only attitude to death in the novel. Catherine has a dream in which:

> heaven did not seem to be my home; and I broke my heart with weeping to come back to earth; and the angels were so angry that they flung me out into the middle of the heath on the top of Wuthering Heights; where I woke sobbing for joy.[20]

Catherine's heaven can be found on the moors and, more specifically, in Wuthering Heights. She has no interest in Heaven, or even in paradise; her mortal home represents her eternal home.

Lockwood expresses a similar philosophy at the end of the novel too:

> I lingered round them, under that benign sky; watched the moths fluttering among the heath and harebells, listened to the soft wind breathing through the grass, and wondered how any one could ever imagine unquiet slumbers for the sleepers in that quiet earth.[21]

Catherine and Lockwood both paint the moors as a heavenly, peaceful existence, totally at odds with Branwell's embarrassment of the crude simplicity of Haworth and his desire to leave it behind and step out onto the world's stage. The fact that these are the last lines of the novel impart a weight and legitimacy to them that suggest they are more than just one character's opinion; they are the author's too. Emily loved the moors and her home, and felt terrible homesickness when she was separated from them.

To Emily the moors represented a paradise, to Branwell a place to escape from. It is inconceivable that he could have written a novel that was so enmeshed in a place he wanted to leave behind.

I fear the *Wuthering Heights* debate has resulted in dismissal and vilification of Branwell for many years now; the suggestion that Emily was not able to write the novel has upset a number of readers, and people can sometimes resort to personal attacks when they're upset.

But I believe I have demonstrated that there should be no such debate; there is no reason to think Branwell wrote *Wuthering Heights*. But even if I haven't convinced you, perhaps I can convince you instead to champion Branwell's poetry rather than argue that he wrote Emily's novel. All of Branwell's published poetry is reproduced at the back of this book, as well as some of his unpublished work. I think you'll find it worthy of being championed, and we'll have better success rehabilitating Branwell this way than arguing over *Wuthering Heights*.

---

1. Emily Brontë, *Wuthering Heights*, (Penguin Popular Classics, 1994) p. 6

2. Emily Brontë, *Wuthering Heights*, (Penguin Popular Classics, 1994) p. 16
3. Francis A. Leyland, *Brontë Family*, (Hurst and Blackett, 1886) p. 186-187
4. Francis Grundy, *Pictures of the Past : Memories of Men I have Met and Places I have Seen* (Griffith and Faran, 1879) p. 80
5. Francis Grundy, *Pictures of the Past : Memories of Men I have Met and Places I have Seen* (Griffith and Faran, 1879) p. 73-74
6. Francis Grundy, *Pictures of the Past : Memories of Men I have Met and Places I have Seen* (Griffith and Faran, 1879) p. 75
7. Francis Grundy, *Pictures of the Past : Memories of Men I have Met and Places I have Seen* (Griffith and Faran, 1879) p. 80
8. Neil Gaiman, *The Sandman: The Wake*, (DC Comics, 1997) p. 159
9. Emily Brontë, *Wuthering Heights*, (Penguin Popular Classics, 1994) p. 151
10. Emily Brontë, *Wuthering Heights*, (Penguin Popular Classics, 1994) p. 136
11. Emily Brontë, *Wuthering Heights*, (Penguin Popular Classics, 1994) p. 155
12. Juliet Barker, *The Brontës* (Abacus, 2010) p. 592
13. The Brontës, *Tales of Glass Town, Angria, and Gondal: Selected Writings*, edited Christine Alexander, (Oxford World's Classics, 2010) p. 399
14. The Brontës, *Tales of Glass Town, Angria, and Gondal: Selected Writings*, edited Christine Alexander, (Oxford World's Classics, 2010) p. 401
15. The Brontës, *Tales of Glass Town, Angria, and Gondal: Selected Writings*, edited Christine Alexander, (Oxford World's Classics, 2010) p. 408
16. Emily Brontë, *Wuthering Heights*, (Penguin Popular Classics, 1994) p. 193
17. Emily Brontë, *Wuthering Heights*, (Penguin Popular Classics, 1994) p. 80
18. Emily Brontë, *Wuthering Heights*, (Penguin Popular Classics, 1994) p. 144
19. Emily Brontë, *Wuthering Heights*, (Penguin Popular Classics, 1994) p. 146-7
20. Emily Brontë, *Wuthering Heights*, (Penguin Popular Classics, 1994) p. 80
21. Emily Brontë, *Wuthering Heights*, (Penguin Popular Classics, 1994) p. 279

WHO IS BRANWELL BRONTË?

GRUNDY DESCRIBED BRANWELL AS 'NO DOMESTIC DEMON – HE WAS JUST a man moving in a mist, who lost his way.'[1]

This is the most (perhaps only) accurate statement Grundy ever made about his friend. The story of Branwell's life paints a picture of a man who felt self-conscious about his origins and himself, tried to live up to a fantasy of how he felt he ought to be, and was ruined as a result.

But the words he left behind paint another picture. Branwell Brontë was an undeniably talented poet (and a terrible novelist). I mentioned at the very beginning of this book that I was exploring who Branwell was, and who is now.

So who is Branwell Brontë to us now?

He's a research opportunity, a chance to gain new or additional insight into the past. I've only scratched the surface; there's a wealth of further research and discussion to be had. For example, there are definite, and very interesting, similarities between Branwell's work and Victorian poetry that are worth exploring.

Branwell is also an insight into the story of atheism. Open atheism was rare in 1800s England, and Branwell is exemplary of how many struggled with their private doubts. His poetry, too, pushes at boundaries, making declarations that were often shocking in their boldness. He deserves to be part of the discussion about atheism in literature at a time when atheism just wasn't acceptable.

Branwell also provides another perspective on the Brontë story, and a reminder that the story we think we know might not be the case. Much of our understanding of the Brontës comes from Charlotte, for instance. We have seen that she wasn't always right when she claimed Branwell wasn't looking for work, dismissed the work he was doing, or offered scathing opinions of his relationship with Lydia Robinson when her own feelings for Monsieur Heger might have encouraged sympathy. Charlotte was also dismissive of Anne, so understanding that she wasn't always right about Branwell bolsters the very worthy opinion that Anne has also been too often overlooked.

Branwell also serves as a cautionary tale against getting wrapped up in your own creations; if he had left behind his fantastical ideas about Byronic heroes, and stopped modeling himself on Alexander Percy, perhaps he might have found better literary success. Even if he had not, the scandalous, ruinous events of his last years have overshadowed his real achievements, and are reason enough to think twice of pretending to be someone we're not.

Finally, Branwell is someone who can proudly step out of the shadows and stand alongside his sisters. He wasn't perfect. He made mistakes. But he was a talented writer, a man who dreamed a little differently, just like his sisters, and a key part of their story.

Branwell is a Brontë.

---

1. Francis Grundy, *Pictures of the Past : Memories of Men I have Met and Places I have Seen* (Griffith and Faran, 1879) p. 92

PART II

THE POEMS OF BRANWELL BRONTË

A NOTE ON THE TEXT

The following is a selection of Branwell's poems. All of his published poetry is included, as well as some examples of his unpublished work. Every poem referred to in previous chapters has been included.

STILL AND BRIGHT, IN TWILIGHT SHINING

Still and bright, in twilight shining,
Glitters forth the evening star;
Closing rosebuds, round me twining,
Shed their fragrance through the air;
Slow the river pales its glancing,
Soft its waters cease their dancing,
Calm and cool the shades advancing
Speak the hours of slumber near!
Why this solemn silence given
To the close of fading day?
Feels the earth the hush of heaven?
Can the expanse of nature pray?
And when daylight's toil is done,
Grateful for summer sunshine gone,
Can it before the Almighty's throne
Its glad obeisance pay?
Such a hush of sacred sadness
Wide around the weary wild,
O'er the whirl of human madness
Spreads the slumbers of a child.

These surrounding sweeps of trees
Swaying to the evening breeze
With a voice like distant seas
Making music mild.
Percy Hall above them lowering,
Darker than the dark'ning sky,
With its halls and turrets towering
Wakes the wind in passing by.
Round that scene of wondrous story
In their old ancestral glory
All its oaks so huge and hoary
Wave their boughs on high.

Among these Turrets there is one
The soonest dark when day is done,
And when Autumn's winds are strongest
Moans the most and echoes longest.
So – on the steps that lie before
A solitary archèd door,
In that lone gable far away
From the sights and sounds of social joy,
Fronting the expanse so dim and grey
There sits a lonely boy.
One hand is in his curling hair
To part it from his brow,
And that young face so soft and fair
Is lifted heavenward now.
On the cold stone he has laid him down
To watch that silver line
Beneath the power of twilight's frown
In the wide west decline.
For heaven still guides his azure eyes
Towards its expanse so wild,
As veiled in darkness there he lies,
A little Angel Child!

Oh who has known, or who can tell
The Fountain of those feelings high
Which, while in this wild world we dwell,
At times will lift us up on high,
In a celestial sympathy
With yon lone vault, yon starry dome,
As if the spirit deemed the sky
Was even on earth its only home,
And while the eye is dim with tears,
The feelings wrapt in dreams sublime,
How dead seem earthly hopes and fears,
How all forgot the soul to time!
And yet the soul can never say
What are the thoughts which make it glow.
We feel they *are*, but *what are* they?
'This this which we must never know
While lingering in this world of woe.

Yet did man's soul descend from heaven
With feelings by its Maker given
All high, all glorious, all divine,
And from his hand perfected gone
With such a bright reflected shine
As the full moon bears from the sun.
But then – the soul was clothed in clay,
So straight its beauty passed away,
And through a whirl of misery driven
Earth's shadow came 'tween it and heaven.
A darkened orb the moon became,
Lost all its lustre, quenched in flame!
Or entering on this morbid life,
The clouds of war, the storms of strife,
Continual passing, veil it round
With gloomy wreaths of shade profound.
So, only shining fitfully,

A single gleam of light we see,
As pass the clouds on either hand
To show the clear calm heaven beyond.
Yet at one moment soars our soul
Into those wayward dreams divine,
Till back again the darkness toll
And hide the uncertain shine.
Yet shall a time come rapid on
When all those clouds that round us frown,
From Heaven's vast vault all past and gone,
Leave the full moon in glory there,
To shine for ever bright and fair.
When this dull clay is cast away
These THOUGHTS shall shine with cloudless ray
And we shall understand what now
[Line undecipherable]
In yon lone child's uplifted eyes
Such dreams can scare be dim,
So late upon those morbid skies
The moon has risen to him;
So late his soul has passed from heaven
That it can scarce forget
The visions bright whose hallowed light
Is round its musings yet.
Silent he sits on the darkened stone,
With night around him rolling,
As if to him that hollow moan
From the old tree tops were calling.
He listens to the eerie wind
Around his Father's dwelling,
Till later following on his mind
More glorious thoughts seem swelling.
For both his little hands were stretched
In rapture to the sky,
When wilder from the wilderness

Each blast came howling by
Towards clouds all southward resting wide
Above the Atlantic sea,
While o'er them far the darksome air
Is haloed lustrously.
He fears some wondrous sight
To him were opening soon,
Till, lo! – that sudden shining light,
'The Moon, the glorious Moon!'

Oh, soft and sweet is the silver beam
That floods the turret high,
While fairy woodlands round it seem
All shining gloriously.
Each window glitters cold and clear
Upon the southern tower,
And – though the shade is darker made
Around his lonely bower –
Yet o'er his face a solemn light
Comes smiling from the sky,
And shows to light the lustre bright
Of his uplifted eye.
The dimless, heedless carelessness
Of happy Infancy,
Yet such a solemn tearfulness
Commingling with his glee,
The parted lips, the shining hair
Cast backward from his brow,
Without a single shade of care,
But bathed amid that moonlight air,
Oh, who so blest as thou!
The moon in glory o'er the grove
Majestic marches on,
With all the vault of heaven above
To canopy her throne;

And from her own celestial rest,
Upon the dark wood's waving crest
Serenely she looks down,
Yet beaming still, as if she smiled,
Most brightly on that beauteous child.
But what thought he as there he lay
Beneath that archèd door,
Amid the ever trembling play
Of moonshine through the bower,
Gazing with blue eyes dimmed with tears
To that vast vault of shining spheres,
Till its mysterious power
Makes the bright drops unnoticed break
In dewy lustre o'er his cheek?

'Oh, how I could wish to fly
Far away through yonder sky,
O'er those trees upon the breeze
To a paradise on high!
Why am I so bound below
That I must not, cannot go,
Lingering here for year on year
So long before I die?
Now how glorious seems to be
Heaven's huge concave stretched o'er me.
But – Every star is hung so far
Away from where I lie.
I love to see that Moon arise –
It suits so well the silent skies.
I love it well, but cannot tell
Why it should make me cry.
Is't that it brings before me now
Those wondrous times gone long ago,
When Angels used from Heaven to come
And make this earth their happy home?

When Moses brought from Egypt's strand
God's favoured tribes through seas and sand
Victorious to the promised land!
When Salem rose, her Judah's pride,
Where David lived and Jesus died!
Is't that I know this very moon
Those vanished wonders gazed upon,
'When Shepherds watched their flocks by night,
All seated on the ground,
And angels of the Lord came down,
And glory shone around?'
Is't that I think upon the sea,
Just now lit beaming beauteously,
Where I so oft have longed to be,
But never yet have been?
Is't that it shines so far away
On Lands beyond that Ocean's spray,
Mong lonely Scotland's hills of grey,
And ENGLAND'S groves of green!
Or is't that through yon deep blue dome
It seems so solemnly to roam,
As if upon some unknown Sea,
A vessel's stately form,
It o'er the waves was wandering free
Through calm and cloud and storm!
I cannot tell but it's in heaven,
And though I view it here
Till I am mouldering dust to dust,
My parted spirit never must
Behold its brightness near.
I am crying to think that mighty throng
Of Glorious Stars to heaven belong,
That they can never, never see
A little earthly child like me;
Still rolling on, still beaming down,

And I unnoticed and unknown,
Though Jesus once in ages gone
Called children to his knee.
So, where he reigns in glory bright
Above these starry skies of night,
Amid his paradise of light,
Oh, why might I not be!
Oft, when awake on Christmas morn,
In sleepless twilight laid forlorn,
Strange thoughts have o'er my mind been borne
How he has died for me;
And oft, within my chamber lying,
Have I awaked myself with crying
From dreams where I beheld him drying
Upon the accursed tree;
And often has my mother said,
While on her lap I laid my head,
She feared for time I was no made,
But for Eternity!
So I can read my title clear
To mansions in the skies,
And let me bid farewell to fear
And wipe my weeping eyes.
I'll lay me down on this marble stone
And set the world aside,
To see upon its ebon throne
Yon moon in glory ride.
I'll strive to pierce that midnight vault
Beyond its farthest star,
Now let my spirit's wanderings halt
'Neath Eden's crystal bar;
For sure that wind is calling me
To a land beyond the grave,
And I must not shrink upon the brink
Of Jordan's heavenly wave;

But I'll fall asleep in its waters deep,
And wake on that blest shore
Where I shall neither want or weep
Or sigh or sorrow more.
Oh, Angels come! Oh, Angels come!
And guide me to my Heavenly Home!'

Guide thee to heaven! – Oh lovely child,
Little knowest thou the tempests wild
Now gathering for thy future years
Their blighting floods of bitter tears.
Little thou knowest how long and dread
Must be thy path ere thou art laid
Within thy dark and narrow bed,
Or how, then, thou wilt shrink to be
Launched out upon Eternity,
All those celestial visions flown,
All Hope of Heaven for ever gone!
This passionate desire for Heaven
Is but the beam of brightness given
Around thy spirit at its birth,
And not yet quenched in clouds of earth,–
The inward yearnings of the soul
Toward its original sad goal,
Before that gial is hid from sight
Amid the gloom of mortal night.
To that just entering into Time
This world is like a stranger clime,
Where – nothing kindred – nothing known
Leaves thy young spirit all alone
To spend its hours in thinking on
The native home whence it has gone.
But – Oh! At last a time will come
When Heaven is lost, and earth is home;
Where pleasures glimmering on thy sight

As soon as seen shall sink in night,
Whilst thou pursuest them through the gloom,
Sinking like willows to the tomb.
This light shall change to lightning then,
This love of Heaven to Hell of men.
So if thou sleekest the glorious name
Thy path shall lead through blood and flame,
From crime to crime, imparting healing,
Blessed thyself and others blessing;
For that which from on high is thrown
Will always fall most rapid down,
And sink the deepest – So with thee,
Thy quick and passionate heart shall be
But farther plunged in misery.
Then those around thee oft may find
Earth and its joys to suit their mind,–
For dust to dust, sons of earth
Will love the land that gave them birth,
Yet never thou, or if thou dost
Full quickly thou shalt find it Dust!

He sleeps! – in slumber calm and deep,
An infant's blest and balmy sleep,
Dreaming of heaven those closèd eyes,
And glorious visions of the skies,
And trembling their fringes lie
On the young cheek of infancy;
The softened curls of golden hair
Just moving in the moonlight air;
But his white brow so sweetly still,
So free from every shade of ill,
Shall it be so for ever? – No!
Who in this world would wish it so.
Yon is the image of a man
Destined to lead the foremost van

Of coming time, and in his hand
The future chooses to command.
'Tis he whose never dying name
Shall see a future world of flame.
PERCY! awake thee from thy sleep.
Awake! to bid thy country weep.

AZRAEL, OR DESTRUCTION'S EVE

Branwell reworked the first forty-eight lines of this poem into 'Noah's Warning Over Methuselah's Grave', which was published in 1842.

'Brothers and men! –One moment stay
Beside your latest patriarch's grave,
While God's just vengeance yet delay–
While Mercy yet have the power to save! –
Now will you force my tongue to say,
That, underneath this nameless sod
Your hands and mine have laid Today
The last on Earth who walked with God!

Shall this pale Corpse whose hoary hairs
Are just surrendered to decay
Dissolve the chain that bound our years
To hundred ages passed away? –
Shall six-score years of warnings dread
Die like a whisper on the wind? –
Shall that dark doom which hangs oer head
Its blinded victims darker find? –

Shall storms from Heaven without the world,
Find wilder storms from Hell within? –
Shall long stored late come wrath be hurled?
Or,–will You–can You, turn from Sin? –
Have patience, if too plain I speak,
For time, My Sons, is hastening by!
Forgive me, if my accents break–
Shall I be saved–and Nature die? –

Forgive that pause!–One look to Heaven
Too plainly tells me He is gone,
Who long with me had vainly striven
For Earth beneath its Makers throne.
He is gone!–My Father, full of days
From life that left no joys for him;
Born in Creation's earliest blaze;
Dying–himself its latest beam!

But–He is gone! and, Oh behold,
Shewn in his death God's latest sign
Than which, more plainly never told
An angel's presence his design. –
By it–the Evening beam withdrawn
Before a starless night descend–
By it–the lastest blest spirit born
From this beginning of an End–
By all the coming strife of war
That brews above yon fated Town–
By all the Hearts worst passions there
That call so loud for Vengeance down. –
By that vast wall of Cloudy gloom,
Surrounding all Heavens firmament–
By all its presages of doom–
Children of Men–Repent! Repent!'

The patriarch ceased, and rung his voice
Like knell of iron from the skies;
But echo none the earth returned
Whose blinded sons with anger burned,
As silent swayed their mighty tide
Around the grave from side to side.
All eyes were bent, with threatening gloom,
On Him who prophesied their doom;
And one arose–upon whose face
Passions and crimes had left their trace,
Contending with a tameless pride
That Man and God alike defied.

'Be Thine,' he cried with trumpet voice
Whole hoarse applauses rolled–'Be Thine
The task to embitter human joys:
To raise, to cherish them, be mine!
Die with the Head that now has died
The miseries of a time gone by;
Descend with him; the Tyrant's pride;
Rise from his ashes, Liberty!
Take him–the type of old things past–
His death–our chain, dissolved at last–
I grant it–take that cloudy gloom
For omen of the storm to come–
Take all thy Types–But know thy age
Looks blindly on life's lettered page.
Dim eyes see darkness even in day,
And wrinkled brows scare smiles away.
Age always thinks the past was bright
And–like itself–deems present, night.
Is't fit that he whose memory fails,
Save when repeating old world tales–
That he who scarce the present knows
Should prophesy of future woes?

'Oh Human Heart! How waywardly
From truth to error thou wilt flee!
We say this world was made by One
Who's seen or heard or known by none.
We say that *He*, the Almighty God
That framed Creation with a nod,
His wondrous works so well fulfilled
That–in an hour–it All rebelled! –
That though He loves our race so well
He hurls our spirits into Hell–
That though He bids us turn from sin
He hedges us, with tempters, in–
That though He says the world shall stand
Eternal–perfect–from His hand,
He is just about to whelm it o'er
With utter ruin–evermore! –
And all for deeds that we have done,
Though He has made us every one–
Yes, We–the image of His form! –
We! –The dust to feed the worm!

'Away with all such phantasies! –
Just trust your reason and your eyes! –
Believe that God exists when I
Who, here–this hour–His name deny,
Shall bear a harder punishment
Than those whose knees to him have bent,
Believe that He can rule above
When you shall see Him rule below;
Believe that He's the God of love
When He shall end His children's woe;
Believe that this firm earth we tread,
And that vast canopy overhead–
Believe that they have stood for ever,
And that they shall for ever stand–

Till something *really* try to sever
The earth from Heaven–the sea from land.
Believe that hoar descending hairs
Are far more sage than youthful years,
When rotting planks shall prove to be
More fruitful than a forest tree.
Old Man! –a truce to dotard dreams,
And turn from Heaven thy hazy eyes–
A Thought for Earth far more beseems
Than childish gazing at the skies,
'Tis Earth–not Heaven–shall shortly rise;
'Tis Man–not God–shall soon avenge;
And if there be a paradise
We'll bring it in the coming change! –
To-morrow morn, my country-men,
We meet within that City's wall–
Let us our Liberty regain–
Be that the "Breaking of our chain"–
Then if all Heaven its terrors rain
We'll smile upon them all!'

As Azrael ceased, throughout the throng
Uprose a tumult loud and long
That howled about the Man of God
And laughed his sorrowing looks to scorn;
Nor could he speak one warning word
Away by surging thousands borne.
One look he cast–one withering look
At Azrael, whose triumphant eye
Could scarce withstand its mute rebuke,
Even in his hour of Victory.
Then swayed the tide on either side,
And each apart were sundered wide;
But o'er the thousands Azrael's form
Shone like a Beacon through a storm;

And o'er the tumult of Azrael's voice
Swelled like a trumpet through the skies.
On toward the wall he bade them tend,
And fast the concourse hurried on,
Forgot Methuselah's burial stone,
Where only Noah mourned alone
Above his father and his friend!

Why walks within his palace hall
Lord Azrael, silent and alone,
While back its roof of marble stone
Returns his footstep's measured fall?–
Why gathers in his restless eye
A shadow of such troubled meaning–
Why, sometimes at the window leaning
So anxious looks he on the sky?–
Why comes so sad the evening down?–
Why sleeps so dark the Mighty town? –
And why *does* every palace dome
Seem mourning 'mid the misty gloom,
While the wind whistles wild and low
About each pillared portico? –
'Twas but an hour since thousands roared
For Azrael o'er Methuselah's grave;
Then why is He, so late adored,
Untended by a single Slave? –
His ears yet ring with uproar loud,
The Applauses of a maddened crowd;
He has left the streets choked up with men
Whose shouts might call him back again.
Alone, he has left them, but his eye
Shows that his mind has company;
And, pacing o'er the dark'ning floor,
On mighty thoughts he seems to pour.
At length, the solemn silence breaking,

As if a Spirit heard him speaking,
So cleaned his hands, so fixed his look,
So earnest every word he spoke.

Azrael (solus loquitur):
'There is no God–I know there's none!
Neither of spirit nor of stone;
No Holy Hill nor Idol Shrine
Has ever held a Power Divine;
Nor Heaven above *nor hell* below
Can minister to weal or woe! –
I feel that when the Body dies
Its memories and feeling die;
That they from earth shall never rise,
As it in earth shall ever lie:
I know that Mortal eyes incline,
Whenever aught remains unseen,
With phantoms dreadful or divine
To people the mysterious scene;
That Human life revolts to think
It ever stands on nothing's brink;
That Human pride recoils to see
The Heap of dust 'tis doomed to be! –
I know that if I staid till night
Alone in this unlighted Hall
My mind would fill with many a sight
The vacuum of the midnight wall;
But–when the Morning light shall rise
The *real* would banish phantasies.
So, when the shadow of TO COME
Surrounds the Heart with boding gloom,
Nature abhors to look at naught
And frames, for ease, a world of thought.
So–when the sick man lies to die
He gasps for Hope in Agony;

And as the Earth yields none to save
He makes a Hope beyond the grave! –
Thus Heaven is but an earthly dream:
'Tis Man makes God–not God makes him!

'But why should I of others speak,
As if all minds but mine were weak? –
We are all the same and each one tries
To cheat his sense with phantasies–
Weak as the weakest–now, even now
When conquest almost crowns my brow,
When with a word I cheer or check
The crowd that follows at my beack,
When those I hated fear my name
And those I feared are bowed with shame,
When, though I tread on Hostile laws,
Am welcomed with the world's applause–
Yet, all avails not! –There is still
A sickening sense of future ill;
Of what I love about to be
A part of what has ceased to be! –
For, I may rise to sovereign sway,
But–MARAH must descend to clay.
To-morrow night must bring me power,
But–*this may* bring her dying hour.
To me a Throne–To her a Tomb–
Fleeting light–And fixed gloom!
Well, so arise, through each one's life,
From laughter, tears–from feasting, strife;
And Earth is not–as some have said–
From Chaos but *to* Chaos made.

'Sometimes I think this inward pain
Is but the ferment of the brain,
Which on this eve of mighty things,

While all is doubt, vain phantoms brings
To fill the void–But comes anon
Death, the real phantom, striding on,
Which, if with wine I drive away,
From merry night comes mournful day.
At night I drive the tumult on,
Pledging healths to lose my own;
Or bask in light from beauties' eyes,
Which I enjoy–and then despise!
At morn, I rise with head confused
To work neglected, food refused,
Until my mind reverts on schemes
To realize a traitor's dreams;
Until the day brings forth again
The evil thoughts of restless men,
Who me their leader hurry on
Towards the deed that *must* be done;
And while their minds my own employ
My heart can feel a troubled joy;
But, if my thoughts a moment roam
Towards what should be my happy home,
Then, oh, my Marah, comes the shade
Of hopes beclouded, joys decayed!
Then I feel that I must be
Soon–how soon! –deprived of Thee!'

There Azrael stopped with bated breath
As if he saw the face of death;
But while he stood there–on his sight,
Between him and the darkened wall,
Behold! a Lady clothed in white
With frightened haste swept through the hall.
Her face and lips were pale as death–
Her glassy eyes were fixed on him–
She strove to speak but gasped for breath

Like one oppressed with goblin dream;
But Azrael cried–'Good God! Is't THOU? –
Marah, my love! What ails thee now?'
She answered–but he scarce *might* hear
Her words, so faint and chilled they were–
She said–'I've risen, who never thought to rise–
Death has unclasped–a little space–
The strictness of his cold embrace,
That I may warn thee ere this body dies–
I've seen–Oh Azrael!'
There her gaze
Went wildly round, while Azrael caught
Her almost falling in the maze
Of some strange scene or stunning though,
And back his clasp her senses brought;
For, once more wildly gazing round,
She said, with awed and solemn sound,
'I've seen God rise from His Eternal Throne
And say–"Bring Mercy *back*–be Vengeance done!"
Then every Angel stooped his golden wing
Before that voice divine
That utter darkness seemed to bring,
Even over Heaven's unutterable shine!
Azrael–I lay alone in bed,
Composing, in my silent room,
My mind to meet its coming doom,
When, lo! a Holy Angel came
And opened to my dimming sight
That scene terrifically bright–
All Heaven–revealed like a wide world of flame.
Oh! Then I heard that dread command,
Which bowed with awe that shining band;
While wide the Angel of Destruction spread
His midnight winds and from the Presence sped
Bent on the deed of doom–

All, all is o'er!
And this wide world will never brighten more,
Nor joy be seen again!
A thousand Storms are waiting for the word,
And when its deep, commencing peal is heard,
Over this heedless Earth they'll spread a shoreless main
My mourning Angel told me I must go
Before begins the march of woe;
Called where the blest in glory reign:
The *last* on earth who may to Heaven attain!
So I must bid farewell to thee,
Doomed to so dread–
Oh God! I cannot speak!
This miserable heart will break
For–NONE WILL HEAR!'

She sickened in his arms–
On his broad breast declined her head,
And strayed her hair;
All sense of feeling fled,
And blighted all her charms!
'She raves,' Lord Azrael said, 'Her brain
Is dizzied with her dying pain.'
So, on a couch her form he laid,
And called her servants–all dismayed
To find their Lady–when, so nigh
All knew the hour when she should die–
Arisen unhelped, and lying there,
They knew not how–but whispers fraught with fear
Passed as they bore her to the bed
Where, decked for death, she erst had laid.

They left Lord Azrael wrapt in thought–
His restless schemes for once forgot,
For once declined his haughty brow,

His haughty hopes for once laid low;
For though he strove to scoff away
All he had just heard Marah say,
It would not go–Methuselah's tomb,
And aged Noah's warning cry,
And that strange night of utter gloom,
Those gathering clouds, that boding sky,
That mournful wind bewailing by,
All fell upon him in that hour
With Nightmare-weight and stunning power.
But, while in sorrows lost, his mind
Was wandering into years behind,
A hand was placed upon his arm
And he turned round with vague alarm
Of some new ill–But, at his back,
Lo, Moloch! –with a treacherous eye
Glinting with false hilarity
Beneath his eyebrows broad and black–
Ah, Tiger heart! that jesting mien
Hides naught but bitterness and sin:
Then each of Hell a worthy brother,
Azrael and Moloch face each other.
'Ha, Azrael! sure that dotard's preaching
Has waked, at last, thy erring heart;
And, softened by his heavenly teaching,
Thou hast ta'en the better part:
Nonsense! leave your saintly sighs;
Fill that goblet–and, be wise!'

'But Marah's dying!' –
'Tell me not so,
When crowns and thrones are waiting on her:
A Crown will cheat both death and woe,
And women best love pomp and honour.
But, what *is* sighing–what is death?

Why, too much or too little breath!
I laugh to think what fools we are
To pull unmeasured jaws at care,
When just a simple glass of wine
Will drive the demon power of evil
To his and our good lord, the Devil!
Come, drink this draught and–feel divine!'

Lord Azrael, at his *fiend's* command,
The goblet seized with shaking hand,
And while at heart the tempter laughed
Deep and devotedly he quaffed;
And with more flushed but brighter brow
Said grimly–'To our *business* now!
To-morrow night must pleasure gay
From all but us drive care away;
But, oh! *with us* to-morrow night
Come counsel black and genius bright.
Then let our stateliest beauties bloom
Like roses round an open tomb;
Then let our Monarch think his power
Stands firmest in its latest hour,
Let MIDNIGHT end his dream! –Let night bring morn
To us brave hearts! from darkness born!
Remember–That to-morrow night
Our Hate, our Tyrant means to join,
With *Thy* dear SARA'S looks of light,
His faltering form and soul supine.
Remember–All his nobles' eyes
Will gaze upon the sacrifice,
When she must say, with voice divine,
To that old Dotard, 'I am thine!'
Remember–To the Royal Court
His sycophants will all resort,
While Cain and Haman mean to vie

'Neath their proud roofs with Majesty,
And all the citizens prepare
To feast beneath the midnight air,
But–the dark lanes–the alleys vile–
On what will *they* be bent the while?
Will their grim brows shine bright with joy?
Yes–with the longing to destroy!
Yes–they *will* join the festival!
Yes–they *will* visit each proud hall!
Here's to their health! Soon may I see
Their naked arms and matted hair,
Tossing aside festivity–
Frighting the rose from faces fair–
Stunning the music-laden air;
And–where they gather–We'll be there!'

He ceased–Each drained another draught;
And Moloch smiled and Azrael laughed;
For laughter waits at trouble's side;
And shouts through cities ta'en by storm–
So–when Lord Azrael saw the wide
Commencing waste assume its form,
Grim gladness buoyed his heart–He took
His comrade's hand and pledged him well,
And spoke a word, and gave a look
That seemed of blood to tell.
They ran o'er many a haughty name,
Marked who should 'scape and who should fall

HEAVEN AND EARTH

Published 5th June 1841 in the Halifax Guardian

Of Earth beneath, a little space
Our eyes at once descry;
But Heaven above us meets our gaze
Like an Infinity.
On *Earth* we see our own abode,
A smoky town, a dusty road,
A neighbouring hull, or grove;
In *Heaven* a thousand worlds of light
Revolving through the gloom of night
O'er endless pathways rove.

While daylight shews this little Earth
It hides the mighty Heaven,
And, but by night, a visible birth
To all the stars is given;
And, fast as fades departing day.
When silent marsh or moorland grey
Mid evening's mist declines,

Then, slowly stealing, star on star,
As night sweeps forward, from afar,
More clear and countless shines.

I know how oft-times clouds obscure them
But, FROM earth ascend
All such vapours drawn before them,
As TO earth they tend;
And when the storms has hastened by,
Upon the earth their ruins lie
Subsided down again,
While Heaven unstained, more glorious glows,
And every star more star-like shews,
"Clear shining after rain."

So thus we view in mortal life.
As circumscribed a scene,
When worthless joys and petty strife
Alone are heard or seen;
But when beyond this life's wild maze,
We let our minds a moment gaze,
How vast the prospects seem!
Not worlds of everlasting light,
But joys on joys celestial bright
In Heaven unbounded gleam.

'Tis day–The day of pomp and power,
Which hides the Heaven divine,
And few will heed in such an hour
How bright its glorious shine;
But when declines youth's summer sun,
When life's last vanities are gone,
Our thoughts from *Earth* are driven;
And, as the shades of Death descend,
How truly seems it's night our friend,

Because–it shews us Heaven.

There's many a grief to shade this scene
And hide those starry skies,
But all such clouds that intervene
From this world will arise;
And, may I smile, O God! to see
Their storms of sorrow beat on me,
When I so surely know
That *Thou* the while art shining on;
That I, at last, when they are gone,
Shall see the glories of thy throne
Beam brighter far than now.

ON THE MELBOURNE MINISTRY

Published 14th August 1841 in the Halifax Guardian. *This is the only poem Branwell published under his own name.*

Men call us worthless, though our deeds,
Since our long reign had birth–
(If any proof our country needs,)
Show *even We* have worth.

Though 'going out,' like dying lamps,
And smelling like them too,
You'll find us good "Adhesive Stamps;"
Or first rate calf-skin glue.

P.B.B.

DEC/19 1841 AT LUDDENDEN CHURCH

O God! while I in pleasures wiles
Count hours and years as one
And deem that wrapt in pleasures smiles
My joys can neer be done

Give me the stern sustaining power
To look into the past
And see the darkly shadowed hour
Which I must meet at last

The hour when I must stretch this hand
To give a last adieu
To those sad friends that round me stand
Whom I no more must view

For false though bright the hours that lead
My present passage on
And when I join the silent dead
Their light will all be gone

Dec/19 1841 at Luddenden Church

Then I must cease to seek the light
Which fires the evening heaven
Since to direct through deaths dark night
Some others must be given

ON LANDSEER'S PAINTING

Published 28th April 1842 in the Bradford Herald

The beams of fame dry up affection's tears;
And those who rise forget from whom they spring;
Wealth's golden glories–pleasure's glittering wing–
All that we follow through our chase of years–
All that hope seeks–all our caution fears,
Dim, or destroy all those holy thoughts, which cling
Round where the forms we loved lie slumbering;
But–not with *thee*–our slave–whose joys and cares
We deem so grovelling–power nor pride are thine,
Nor our pursuits nor ties, yet, o'er this grave,
Where lately crowds the form of mourning gave,
I only hear *thy* low heartbroken whine;
I only see *thee* left, long hours to pine
For *him* whim thou–if love had power–would'st save!

ON THE CALLOUSNESS PRODUCED BY CARES

Published 5th May 1842 in the Bradford Herald *and 7th May 1842 in the* Halifax Guardian

Why hold young eyes the fullest fount of tears;
And why do youthful breasts the oftenest sigh,
When fancied friends forsake, or lovers fly,
Or fancied woes and dangers wake their fears?
Ah! he who asks has seen but spring tide years;
Or Time's rough voice had long since told him why!
Increase of days increases misery,
And misery brings selfishness, which sears
The hearts first feelings: 'mid the battle's roar
In death's dread grasp the soldier's eyes are blind
To comrades dying, and he whose hopers are oer
Turns coldest from the sufferings of mankind:
A bleeding spirit oft delights in gore;
A tortured heart oft makes a tyrant mind.

THE AFGHAN WAR

Published 7th May 1842 in the Leeds Intelligencer

Winds within our chimney thunder,
Rain showers shake each window pane;
Still–if nought our household sunder–
We can smile at wind and rain.
Sickness shades a loved one's chamber;
Steps glide gently, to and fro;
Still–'mid woe, our hearts remember
We are there to soothe that woe.

Comes at last the hour of mourning; –
Solemn tolls the funeral bell; –
And we fell, that no returning
Fate allows to such farewell;
Still, a holy hope shines o'er us,
We, wept by the one who died;
And, 'neath earth, shall death restore us–
As round hearthstones–side by side.

But–when all at ever, together
Circle round the flickering light,
While December's howling weather
Ushers in a stormy night;
When each ear, scarce conscious, listens
To the outside winter's war,
When each trembling eye-lash glistens
As each thinks of *one* afar–

Men to chilly silence dying,
Ceases story, song, and smile;
Thought asks–"Is the loved one lying
Cold, upon some storm-beat isle?"
And, with death–when doubtings vanish,
When despair still hopes and fears;
Though our anguish toil may banish,
Rest brings unavailing tears.

So, Old England–when they warning
Of thy funeral bells I hear,
Though thy dead a host are mourning,
Friends and kindred watch each bier.
But, alas! Atlantic waters
Bear another sound from far!
Unknown woes–uncounted slaughters–
Unwept deaths–inglorious war!

Breasts and banners crushed and gory,
That seemed once invincible;
England's children–England's glory,
Moslem sabres smite and quell.
Far away their bones are wasting,
But I hear their spirits call–
Is our Might Mother hasting
To avenge her children's fall?

England rise! thine ancient thunder
Humbled mightier foes than these;
Broke a whole world's bonds asunder;
Gave thee empire o'er the seas.
And while yet one rose may blossom,
Emblem of thy former bloom,
Let not age invade thy bosom;
Brightest shine in darkest gloom.

While one oak thy homes shall shadow.
Stand like it as thou hast stood;
While a spring greets grove and meadow,
Let not winter freeze thy blood.
'Till this hour St George's standard
Led the advancing march of time.
England! Keep it streaming vanward;
Conqueror over age and clime.

ON PEACEFUL DEATH AND PAINFUL LIFE

Published 12th May 1842 in the Halifax Guardian

Why dost thou sorrow for the happy dead?
For if their life be lost their toils are o'er,
And woe and want can trouble them no more;
Nor ever slept they in an earthly bed
So sound as now they sleep, while dreamless laid
In the dark chambers of the unknown shore,
Where Night and Silence guard each sealed door.
So–turn from such as thee thy drooping head
And mourn the *dead alive*, whose spirit flies,
Whose life departs, before his death has come;
Who knows no Heaven beyond his gloomy skies;
Who sees no Hope to brighten up that gloom:
'Tis he who feels the worm that never dies,
The *real* death and darkness of a tomb!

CAROLINE'S PRAYER

Published 2nd June 1942 in the Bradford Herald *and 4th June 1842 in the* Halifax Guardian

My Father, and my childhood's guide,
If oft I've wandered far from thee;
Even though thine only son has died
To save from death a child like me.

O! still–to thee when turns my heart,
In hours of sadness–frequent now–
Be thou the God that once thou wert;
And calm my breast, and clear my brow.

I'm now no more a little child
O'ershadowed by thine angel wing,
My very dreams seem far more wild
Than those my slumbers used to bring.

I farther see–I deeper feel–
With hope more warm, but heart less mild,

And former things new shapes reveal,
All strangely brightened or despoiled.

I am entering on Life's open tide;
So–Farewell, childhood's shores divine!
And Oh, my father, deign to guide
Through these wide waters, Caroline!

SONG

Published 9th June 1842 in the Bradford Herald *and 11th June 1842 in the* Halifax Guardian

Should Life's first feeling be forgot,
As Time leaves years behind?
Should Man's for ever changing lot
Work changes on his mind?

Should space, that sever heart from heart,
The heart's best thoughts destroy?
Should years, that bid our youth depart,
Bid youthful memories die?

Oh! say not that these coming years
Will warmer friendships bring;
For friendship's joys and hopes and fears
From deeper fountains spring.

Its feelings to the *heart* belong;
Its sign–the glistening eye;

While new affections, on the *tongue*
Arise, and live, and die.

So, Passing crowds may *smiles* awake,
The passing hour to cheer;
But–only old acquaintance' sake
Can ever wake a *tear*.

AN EPICUREAN'S SONG

Published 7th July 1842 in the Bradford Herald *and 7th July 1842 in the* Halifax Guardian

The visits of sorrow,
Say, why should we mourn?
Since the sun of to-morrow
May shine on its urn;
And all that we think such pain
Will have departed–then
Bear for a moment what cannot return:

For past time has taken
Each hour that it gave,
And they never awaken
From yesterday's grave,
So surely we may defy
Shadows, like memory,
Feeble and fleeting as midsummer wave.

From the depths where they're falling,

Nor pleasure, nor pain,
Despite our recalling,
Can reach us again:
Though we brood over them,
Nought can recover them;
Where they are laid they must ever remain.

So seize we the present,
And gather its flowers;
For–mournful or pleasant–
'Tis all that is ours.
While daylight we're wasting,
The evening is hasting,
And night follows fast on the vanishing hours.

Yes–and we, when that night comes–
Whatever betide,
Must die as our fate dooms,
And sleep by their side;
For *change* is the only thing
Always continuing;
And it sweeps creation away with its tide!

ON CAROLINE

Published 12th July 1942 in the Bradford Herald *and 14th July 1842 in the* Halifax Guardian

The light of thy ancestral hall,
Thy Caroline, no longer smiles:
She has changed her palace for a pall;
Her garden walks for Minister aisles.
Eternal sleep has stilled the breast
Which peace and pleasure made their shrine;
The golden head has sunk to rest,
Which used to beam with rays divine.

To thee, while watching o'er the bed
Where mute, and motionless she lay,
How slow the midnight moments sped!
How void of sunlight broke the day!
Nor oped her eyes to morning's beam,
Though all around thee woke but her;
Nor oped thy raven pinioned dream
Of coffin, shroud, and sepulchre.

On Caroline

Why beats they breast when hers is still?
Why lingerest thou when she is gone?
Hopest thou to light on good in ill?
To find companionship, alone?
Perhaps thou think'st the church-yard stone
Will hide past smiles, and bury sighs;
That memory, with her soul, has flown;
That thou can'st leave her where she lies?

No! joy *itself* is but a shade,
So well may its *remembrance* die;
But cares–life's conquerors–never fade,
So strong is their reality!
Thou mayest forget the day which gave
That child of beauty to thy side,
But, not the moment when her grave,
Took back again thy borrowed bride!

NOAH'S WARNING OVER METHUSELAH'S GRAVE

Published 25th August 1842 in the Bradford Herald

Brothers and men! One moment stay
Beside your latest patriarch's grave,
While God's just vengeance yet delay–
While God's blest mercy yet can save.

Will you compel my tongue to say,
That underneath this nameless sod
Your hands, with mine, have laid to-day
The *last* on earth who walked with God?

Shall his pale corpse, whose hoary hair
Are just surrendered to decay,
Dissolve the chain which bound our years
To hundred ages passed away?

Shall six-score years of warnings dread
Die like a whisper on the wind?
Shall the dark doom above your head,

Its blinded victims darker find?

Shall storms from heaven *without* the world,
Find wilder storms from hell, *within*?
Shall long stored–late come wrath be hurled;
Or–will you–can you turn from sin?

Have patience if too plain I speak,
For time, my sons, is hastening by;
Forgive me if my accents break;
Shall I be saved and *Nature* die?

Forgive that pause:–One look to Heaven
Too plainly tells me He is gone,
Who, long, with me in vain had striven
For earth, beneath its Maker's throne.

He is gone!–My Father–full of days–
From life which left no joy for him;
Born in creation's earliest blaze;
Dying–himself, its latest beam.

But he gone! And, oh, behold,
Shewn in his death, God's latest sign!
Than which more plainly never told
An angel's presence, his design.

By it, the evening beams withdrawn
Before a starless night descend;
By it, the last blest spirit born
From this beginning of an end!

By all the strife of civil war
That beams within yon fated town;
By all the hearts worst passions there,

That call so loud for vengeance down;

By that *vast* wall of cloudy gloom,
Piled round heaven's boding firmament;
By all its presages of doom,
Children of men–Repent! Repent!

THE EMIGRANT–TWO SONNETS

Published 7th June 1845 in the Yorkshire Gazette

When sink from sight the landmarks of our home,
And–all the bitterness of farewell's o'er–
We yield our spirit unto ocean's foam,
And, in a new-born life which lies before,
On far Columbian or Austalian shore,
Strive to exchange time past for time to come;
How melancholy then–if morn restore
(Less welcome than the night's forgetful gloom)
Old England's blue hills to our sight again;
When we, our thoughts seemed weaning from her sky,
That *pang*, which wakes the almost silenced pain!
Thus, when the sick man lies resigned to die,
A well-loved voice, a well-remembered strain,
Lets time break harshly in upon eternity.

When, after his long day consumed in toil

'Neath the scare welcome shade of unknown trees,
Upturning thanklessly in a foreign soil,
The lonely exile seeks his evening ease–
'Tis not those tropic woods his spirit sees;
Nor calms, to him, that heaven this earth's turmoil,
Nor cools his burning brow that spicy breeze,
Ah, no! the gusty clouds of England's isle
Bring music waften on their stormy wind,
And welcome gleams the little daisy flower;
While "Auld Lang Syne" the darkness calls to mind.
Thus when the demon Thirst, beneath his power
The wanderer bows–to feverish sleep consigned,
He hears the rushing rill and feels the cooling shower.

ON LANDSEER'S PICTURE

Published 10th May 1845 in the Yorkshire Gazette

The blaze of fame dries up affection's tears,
And those who rise forget from whom they spring;
Wealth's golden glories–pleasure's glittering wing–
All that man chases through his whirl of years–
All that his heart seeks–all his caution fears
Dazzle of drown the holy thoughts that cling
Round where the form he loved lies slumbering;
But not with *Thee*–poor slave, whose joys or cares
Man deems so worthless–power nor pride are thine,
Or man's pursuits or ties; –yet o'er this grave
Where crowds, so late the form of mourning gave
I only hear thy low heart-broken whine–
I only see thee left, long hours to pine
For him whom thou (if love had power) wouldst save.

BLACK COMB

Published 10th May 1845 in the Yorkshire Gazette

Far off, and half revealed 'mid shade and light,
Blackcomb half smiles, half frowns; his mighty form
Scarce blending into peace; –more formed to fight
A thousand years of struggles with a storm
Than bask one hour, subdued by sunshine warm
To bright and breezeless rest; –yet even *his* height
Towers not o'er this world's sympathies–he smiles,
While many a human heart to pleasure's wiles
Can bear to bend, and still forget to rise;
As though he, huge and heath clad, on our sight,
Again rejoices in his stormy skies,
Man loses vigour in unstable joys.
Thus tempests find Black Comb invincible,
While we are lost, who should know life so well!

LYDIA GISBORNE

'Gisborne' was Lydia Robinson's maiden name. Branwell also scribbled "Lydia B–" in the margins of this poem.

On Ouses grassy banks – last Whitsuntide,
I sat, with fears and pleasures, in my soul
Commingled, as "it roamed, without control,"
Oer present hours and through a future wide
Where love, methought, should keep, my heart beside
Her, whose own prison home I looked upon:
But, as I looked, descended summer's sun,
And did not its descent my hopes deride?
The sky though blue was soon to change to grey –
I, on that day, next year must own no smile –
And as those waves, to Humber far away,
Were gliding – so, though that hour might beguile
My Hopes, they too, to woe's far deeper sea,
Rolled past the shores of Joy's now dim and distant isle.

REAL REST

Published 8th November 1845 in the Halifax Guardian

I see a corpse upon the waters lie,
With eyes turned, swelled and sightless, to the sky,
And arms outstretched, to move as wave on wave
Upbears it in its boundless billowy grave.
Not Time, but Ocean thins its flowing hair;
Decay, not sorrow, lays its forehead bare;
Its members move, but not in thankless toi,
For seas are milder than this world's turmoil;
Corruption robs its lips and cheeks of red,
But wounded vanity grieves not the dead;
And, though these members hasten to decay,
No pang of suffering takes their strength away;
With untormented eye, and heart, and brain,
Through calm and storm it floats across the main:
Though love and joy have perished long ago,
Its bosom suffers not one pang of woe;
Though weeds and worms its cherished beauty hide,
It feels not wounded vanity or pride;

Though journeying towards some far off shore,
It needs no care or purse to float it o'er;
Though launched in voyage for Eternity
It need not think upon what it is *to be*;
Though naked, helpless, and companionless,
It feels not poverty or knows distress.
Oh corpse! If thou could'st tell my aching mind
What scenes of sorrow thou hast left behind;
How sad the life which, breathing, thou hast led,
How free from strife thy sojourn with the dead;
I could assume thy place–could long to be
A world-wide wanderer oer the waves with thee!
I have a misery where thou hast none;
My heart beats bursting while thine lies like stone;
My veins throb wild while thine are dead and dry;
And woes, not waters, dim my restless eye:
Thou longest not with one well loved to be,
And absence does not break a chain with thee:
No sudden agonies dart through thy breast;
Thou hast what all men covet, REAL REST.
I have an outward frame unlike to thine,
Warm with young life–not cold in death's decline;
An eye that sees the sunny light of heaven–
A heart by please thrilled–by anguish riven–
But in exchange for thy untroubled calm,
Thy gift of cold obvlivions healing balm,
I'd give my youth–my health–my life to come,
And share thy slumbers in thy ocean tomb.

PENMAENMAWR

Published 20th December 1845 in the Halifax Guardian

These winds, these clouds, this chill November storm
Bring back again thy tempest-beaten form
To eyes that look upon yon dreary sky
As, late, they looked on thy sublimity,
When I, more troubled than thy restless sea,
Found, on its waves, companionship with thee.
'Mid mists thou frownest over Arvon's shore–
'Mid tears I watched thee over ocean's roar–
And thy blue front, by thousand storms laid bare,
Claimed kindred with a heart worn down by care.
No smile hadst thou, o'er smiling fields aspiring,
And none had I, from smiling scenes retiring;
Blackness, 'mid sunlight, tinged thy slaty brow,
I, mid sweet music, looked as dark as thou;
Old Scotland's song, o'er murmuring surges born,
Of "times departed–never to return,"
Was echoed back in mournful tones from thee,
And found an echo, quite as sad, in me:

Waves, clouds and shadows moved in restless change
Around, above, and on thy rocky range,
But seldom aw that sovereign front of thine
Changes more quick than those which passed o'er mine!
And as wild winds and human hands, at length
Have turned to scattered stones the mighty strength
Of that old fort, whose belt of boulders grey,
Roman or Saxon legions held at bay,
So had, methought, the young unshaken nerve
That, when WILL wished, no doubt could cause to swerve,
That on its vigour ever placed reliance–
That to its sorrows sometimes bade defiance,
Now left my spirit, like thyself, old hill,
With head defenceless against human ill;
And, as thou long hast looked upon the wave
That takes, but gives not, like a churchyard grave,
I, like life's course, through either's weary range,
Never know rest from ceaseless strife and change.
But, PENMAENMAWR, a better fate was thine
Through all its shades, than that which darkened mine.
No quick thoughts thrilled through thy gigantic mass
Of woe for what might be, or is, or was:
Thou hads't no memory of the glorious hour
When Britain rested on thy giant power:
Thou has'st no feeling for the verdant slope
That leant on thee as man's heart leans on hope:
The pastures, chequered o'er with cot and tree,
Though tho wert Guardian, got no smile from thee;
Old Ocean's wrath their charm might overwhelm,
But thou could'st still keep thy unshaken realm–
While I felt flashes of an inward feeling,
As fierce as those thy craggy form revealing
In nights when blinding gleams and deafening roar
Hurls back thy echo to old Mona's shore.
I knew a flower whose leaves were meant to bloom

Till Death should snatch it to adorn the tomb,
Now, blanching 'neath the blight of hopeless grief
With never blooming and yet living leaf;
A flower on which my mind would wish to shine,
If but one beam could break from mind like mine:
I had an ear whuch could on accents dwell
That might as well say "perish" as "farewell"
An eye which saw, far off, a tender form
Beaten, unsheltered, by affliction's storm–
An arm–a lip–that trembled to embrace
And Angel's gentle breast and sorrowing face–
A mind that clung to Ouse's fertile side
While tossing–objectless–on Menai's tide!
Oh soul! That draw'st yon mighty hill and me
Into communion of vague unity,
Tell me, can I obtain thy stony brow
That fronts the storm, as much unbroken brow
As when it one upheld the fortress proud,
Now gone, like its own morning cap of cloud?
Its breast is stone. Can I have one of steel,
Tendure–inflict–defend–never feel?
It stood as firm when haughty Edward's word,
Gave hill and dale to England's fire and sword,
As when white sails and steam-smoke tracked the sea,
And all the world breathed peace, but waves and me.
Let me, like it, arise o'er mortal care;
All evils bear, yet never know despair;
Unshrinking face the griefs I now deplore,
And stand, through storm and shine, like moveless
PENMAENMAWR.

LETTER FROM A FATHER ON EARTH TO HIS CHILD IN HER GRAVE

Published 18th April 1846 in the Halifax Guardian

From Earth, –whose life-reviving April showers
Hide winter's withered grass 'neath springtide flowers,
And give, in each soft wind that drives the rain,
Promise of fields and forests green again–
I write to thee, the aspect of whose face
Can never change with change of time or place;
Whose eyes could look on India's wildest wars
More calmly than the hardiest son of Mars;
Whose lips, more firm than Stoic's long ago,
Would neither smile with joy nor blanch with woe;
Whose limbs could sufferings far more firmly bear
Than could heroic sinews strung for war;
Whose frame desires no good, nor shrinks from ill,
Nor feels distraction's throb nor pleasure's thrill.
I write words to thee which thou wilt not read,
For thou wilt slumber on howe'er may bleed
The heart, which many think a worthless stone,
But which oft aches for its beloved one;

Nor, if God's life mysterious, from on high
Gave, once gain, expression to thine eye,
Would'st thou thy father know, or feel that he
Gave life, and lineaments, and thoughts to thee,
For, when thou diest, thy day was in its dawn,
And night still struggled with life's opening morn;
The twilight star of childhood, thy young days
Alone illumined, with its twinkling rays,
So sweet, yet feeble; given from those dusky skies,
Whose kindling, future noontide prophesies,
But tells us not that brightest noon may shroud
Our sunshine with a sudden veil of cloud.
If, when thou gavest back the life which ne'er
To thee had given either hope or fear,
But peacefully had passed, nor asked if joy
Should cheer thy future path, or grief annoy–
If, then, thoud'st seen, upon a summer sea
One, once in features, as in blood like thee
On skies of azure blue and waters green
Commingled in the midst of summer's sheen,
Hopelessly gazing–ever hesitating
'Twixt miseries, every hour fresh fears creating
And joys–whate'er they cost–still doubly dear–
Those "troubled pleasures soon chastised by fear"–
If thou hadst seen him thou wouldst ne'er believe
That thou hadst yet known what it was to live.
Thy eyes could only see thy mother's breast,
Thy feeling only wish on that to rest;
It was thy world; –Thy food and sleep it gave,
And slight the change 'twixt it and childhood's grave.
Thou view'dst this world like one who, prone, reposes
Upon a plain and in a bed of roses
With nought to see save marbled skies above,
Nor hear, expect the breezes in the grove:
I–thy life's source–was a wanderer breasting

Keen mountain winds, and on a summit resting,
Whose rough rocks rose above the grassy mead
With sleet and north winds howling over head,
And nature, like a map, beneath him spread:
Far winding river, tree, and tower, and town,
Shadow and sunlight, 'neath his gaze mark'd down
By that mysterious hand which graves the plan
Of that drear country called the life of man.
If seen, men's eyes would, loathing, shrink from thee,
And turn, perchance, with no disgust from me;
Yet thou had'st beauty, innocence, and smiles,
And now hast rest from this world's woes and wiles,
While I have restlessness and worrying care,
So, sure thy lot if brighter–happier–far!
So may it prove–and, though thy ears may never
Hear these words sound beyond Death's darksome river
Not vainly, from the confines of despair
May rise a voice of joy that THOU art freed from care!

THE END OF ALL

Published 5th June 1847 in the Halifax Guardian

In that unpitying winter's night,
When my own wife–my Mary– died,
I, by the fire's declining light,
Sat comfortless, and silent sighed,
While burst unchecked grief's bitter tide,
As I, methought, when she was gone,
Not hours, but years like this must bide,
And wake, and weep, and watch alone.

All earthly hope had passed away,
And each clock stroke brought death more nigh
To the still chamber where she lay,
With soul and body calmed to die:
But mine was not her heavenward eye
When hot tears scorch'd me, as her doom
Made my sick heart throb heavily
To give impatient anguish room.

"Oh now," methought, "a little while
And this great house will hold no more
Her whose fond love the gloom could wile
Of many a long night gone before!
Oh! all those happy hours were o'er,
When, seated by our own fire-side,
I'd smile to hear the wild winds roar,
And turn to clasp my beauteous bride."

I could not bear the thoughts which rose,
Of what *had* been, and what *must* be,
And still the dark night would disclose
Its sorrow-pictured prophecy;
Still I saw–miserable me,
Long–long nights else–in lonely gloom,
With time-bleached locks and trembling knee,
Walk aidless–hopeless–to my tomb.

Still, still that tomb's eternal shade
Oppressed my heart with sickening fear,
When I could see its shadow spread
Over each dreary future year,
Whose vale of tears woke such despair
That, with the sweat-drops on my brow,
I wildly raised my hands in prayer
That death would come and take me now:

Then stopped to hear an answer given–
So much had madness warped my mind–
When–sudden–through the midnight heaven–
With a long howl woke the winter's wind;
And roused in me–though undefined–
A gushing thought of tumbling seas
Whose wild waves wandered unconfined,
And, far off surging, whispered "Peace."

I cannot speak the feeling, strange,
Which shewed that vast December sea,
Nor tell whence came that sudden change
From aidless, hopeless misery;
But, somehow, it revealed to me
A life–when things I loved were gone–
Whose solitary liberty
Might suit me, wandering tombward on:

'Twas not that I forgot my love
That night departing evermore–
'Twas hopeless grief for her that drove
My soul from all it prized before,
Till that blast called it to explore
A new-born life, whose stony joy
Might calm the pangs of sorrow o'er, –
Might *shrine* their memory, not *destroy*.

I rose and drew the curtains back
To gaze upon the starless waste,
And image on the midnight wrack,
The path on which I longed to haste,
From storm to storm continual cast,
And not one moment given to view
O'er minds wild winds the memories, past
Of hearts I loved–of scenes I knew.

My mind anticipated all
The things my eyes have seen since then–
I heard the trumpet's battle-call–
I rode o'er ranks of bleeding men–
I swept the waves of Norway's main–
I tracked the sands of Syria's shore–
I felt that such strange strife and pain
Might me from living death restore.

Ambition, I could make my bride,
And joy to see her robed in red,
For none through blood so wildly ride
As those whose hearts before have bled;
Yes–even though THOU shouldst long have laid
Pressed coldly down by churchyard clay,
And though I knew thee, thus decayed,
I *might* smile grimly, when away–

Might give an opiate to my breast–
Might dream: –but oh! that heart-wrung groan,
Forced from me, with the thought confessed
That all would go if SHE were gone:
I turned, and wept, and wandered on
All restlessly–from room to room–
To that still chamber, where, alone,
A sick-light glimmered through the gloom:

There, all unnoticed time flew o'er me
While my breast bent above her bed,
And that drear life which loomed before me
Choked up my voice–bowed down my head–
Sweet holy words to me she said,
Of that bright heaven which shone so near,
And oft and fervently she prayed
That I might, sometime, meet her there;

But, soon enough, all words were over
When this world passed, and paradise,
Through deathly darkness, seemed to hover
O'er her halfdull–half brightening eyes–
One last dear glance she gives her lover,
One last embrace before she dies,
And then, while he seems bowed above her
His MARY sees him from the skies.

SPEAK KINDLY

Published 19th September 1846 in the Halifax Guardian. *There is some debate as to whether this poem is Branwell's or Emily's. Emily isn't known to have published in any papers, but neither were any of Branwell's poems without a signature, be it his own or Northangerland's. The poem reads like Branwell's, though, which is why I have included it.*

Speak kindly to thy fellow man,
Who droops from weight of woe!
He sinks beneath deep sorrow's ban
With cares thou canst not know:
Oh! kindly speak, for deadly grief
Is gnawing at his heart;
It may be thine to give relief,
And act a brother's part!

Perchance, from thee, a single word,
Spoken in accents kind,
May a sweet transient joy afford
To his o'ercharged mind;
And though his careworn heart is filled

With heaviness and gloom,
It may cause peace and hope to gild
His passage to the tomb!

Turn not the wanderer away,
E'en though the weight of sin
Hath quench'd his spirit's heavenly ray,
And darken'd all within!
Oh! chide him not–nor coldly spurn
His now repentant tears;
For from that one good spark may burn
A flame in after years!

Yes! kindly speak–and bid his soul
From its dejection rise,
Push back the waves which round him roll,
And point him to the skies:
Stay not to ask his grade, nor how
He into evil ran, –
It is enough for thee to know
He is thy fellow man.

THINK NOT THAT LIFE IS HAPPINESS

Think not that life is happiness,
But deem it duty joined with care.
Implore for hope in your distress,
And for your answers get Despair.
Yet travel on, for Life's rough road
May end, at last, in rest with GOD.

PART III

AND THE WEARY ARE AT REST BY BRANWELL BRONTË

the lap against which my temples used to beat was not that of a Mother or daughter but of a WIFE and if I appear outwardly forgetful of her now do I not inwardly think of her till sleep snatches away remembrance? I have no longer the half bashful half delighted cheek to blush to my morning salutations no longer the evening solace for the past days cares but of those cares themselves I have plenty who as each fresh one enters my bosom bring tidings of others on the road and if this strong Frame and iron constitution of mine fail me—Good God! What should I do! I dread a single hint at physical decay as the criminal does each tick of the clock which must toll his knell. When this firm foot can no longer tread the heather this warm blood no longer thrill to a womans touch this working brain no longer teem with thick coming fancies this omnivourous stomach no longer bear its three bottles or twenty tumblers—then what the devil is Alexander Percy to do? I am not a woman to bear pain with patience so the life of an invalid would kill me or drive me mad. Fancy ME reclining on four pillows—attended by as many nurses—the pill and the draught my only nourishment—the physician and the surgeon my only friends—cares for a decaying body my employment for this life—My Vicar or his curate the gate posts to flank me in an Harlequin jump into the life to come No Mary—No, nor Thee Maria—to remind me by their voice and presence that earth has had its 'Paradise lost'; no Ezekiel or Zechariah or Habbakuk or other hero with a name as rough as his beard to give me a shoulder hitch into 'Paradise regained.' Well as honest Nym has it "things must be as they may' So for this days work I shall begin with some sport—secondly get up a row—thirdly excite a fever in my veins by an hours talk with yonder neglected lady—fourthly excite one in the veins of my companions by rapid communication with Thurstons wine cellar—fifthly go to bed in as bad a temper as a badger after a baiting and sixthly rise from bed with another step advanced toward the bodily ruin I so abhorr. Well as Nym again has it "Conclusions must pass"—Hallo! Bob you rascal did I not swear I would kick you down to your last master if I found you drunk this morning—What are you bullying Thurston for? But you shall have my boots presently."

So saying and in no very hesitating accent Mr Percy jumped over the gully which divided him from the shooting party gathering round the fire, and collared his little old servant who had been standing opposite to the Lord of the manor with most un—menial assurance, while Mr Thurston looked on the groom with a scowl which was transfered on Percy's advent to the grooms master.

"What is this old horse stealer about Thurston?" asked Mr Percy giving Bob a shake that discomposed his stomach—

"Oh Sir—ask your servant yourself—for I'm damned if I care."

"Thurston let me have none of your ill humours shewn or I'll send you to the Leeds Infirmary to be tapped—Now Robert le Diable—"

"Aw cannot spake Maister—yaw throttle me so."

"Lie the first—now go on you old fool—Hector do not you interfere."

"Weel Maister" said the old man liberated from the gripe of his gigantic young Master—and putting on the mask of one grievously wronged though much forgiving—"Weel Aw will just tell all as straight as t' Craven Heifer's back and as fast as the winner o' th' Leger—Weel Aw hev been yaw're sarvent and the sarvent o' yaw're father—and knew him that wor th' owd maister of all— and hev donced you on me knees and gein ye th' first pack of cairds you handled—and leughed when yaw teuk th' Jack up and said he wor a sweet un and" —Here the old patriarch wiped one eye with his coat cuff but the clenched and whitened knuckles of his masters fist moved him to restrain his more tender feelings—"Weel—Aw niwer wor so behaved tull sin' aw wor wick and walking! Aw can stand somemut to sup on, but Aw can not stand a lee!—This Gentleman says Aw wor seen wi' a lady in his plantation this varry morning and Aw can tak my awn owd family Bible to witness that Aw nivver melled wi' no lasses niwer sin' aw wor born into this wearisome warld!"

Thurston himself could not help a grim smile at the old scoundrels denial of attempts at flirtation but all smile on his face died as soon as born so he grimly asked Percy

"Are we going to lose our sport for your impudent old groom?"

"Oh no Thurston—time enough yet—now Bob my Vestal virgin —go on!"

"Weel Maister he says he see'd me wi' his awn cousin—Miss—Aw do not kmow what they call her."

"Miss Allen Bob—well go on lad—"

"And he said he saw thee kiss her" roared Mr Montmorency in high apparent glee at the farce enacting—

"Silence Hector as you value that front tooth—" exclaimed Percy rather seriously.

"Naw Maister Aw tak the blessed book or owd John Wesleys hymns or ought else yaw like to witness that Aw wor there and then filling yawr hampers and feeding yawre dogs—for Me—me thats gotten to age Aw hev getten to—to be called a follower o' women is railly—nay—it's beyont raison!"

"Now Percy" broke in Mr Thurston "I must stop this humbug—I did see from my dressing room window that fellow of yours pass to and from one of my relations—I mean a yong lady in my house as if on a message or by appointment—and I afterwards saw a Gentleman whom Montmorency saw like wise and affirms was yourself enter into the thicket—Come aside Percy—I want to talk to you."

"Not a step from this spot will I stir William—I'll have this cleared up before I walk a stride or fire a shot!"

Mr Percy's brow darkened into the hue almost of Thurstons as he laid down his fowling piece and turning to Mr Montmorency asked—

"Now Hector—this day shall either prove sport or earnest—Which do you wish it to be—I ask Thurston as well as yourself and can tell you I am ready for either—"

"For sport—I should have said my dearest" chuckled the Barrister—"But if we stay here much longer we shall have a glut of that sort of thing—We shall need earnest to vary the entertainment. Two Squires quarrelling over a drunken servant about a mornings dream! Pray God they do not shoot each other instead of moor cocks."

"Hector my old fellow I am not just in the humour to be manufactured into either a cricket bat or ball or wicket I wish neither to strike—be the means of striking or be struck but I am—if as innocent looking as arsenic—just as dangerous, and look at this"—here Mr Percy dashed a charge of powder from his flask into his palm—"There is stuff that can keep quiet for twenty yearrs but if kept carefully mark you—only wants one snap of that trigger to send to Hell King Solomon in all his glory"

"Aye—its pretty powder—Its like thy temper Percy—short and sudden and like friend Thurstons face—black and ugly"

"Come aside Percy—I want to talk to you" said Thurston breaking in on the conversation "And I say Alexander You must come or I'll take care we do not make a pleasant day of it though I am your host—"

The idea that a quarrel with his ill tempered entertainer would just now be very ill timed was cunningly whispered by Montmorency into Percy's ear and readily received by the latter who walked to a short distance with Mr Thurston and then was stopped by the latter who said with a burst of ill temper

"What the devil did you meet Miss Allen for this morning"

"If I did it was as a somnambulist"

"Montmorency says you did"

"Then he lies."

"Your servant I myself saw meet her."

"Thats more than I did"

"But he is your servant and so he must have met her on a message from yourself"

"Thats more than I know"

"Is he not your servant?"

"No—He is my groom but the devils servant"

"Percy you play with edge tools and I will not be baulked by you! Mind what I say—I will not be baulked by you! You know what I mean and either in one case or in another I repeat I will not be baulked by you! I am a man of few words Percy but if I do not say much I think a deal and on occasion I can act—I do not speak threatningly—I regard you as my guest and aquaintance and friend and in fact all that sort of thing—but—why if the truth will out—I have lost a deal of money and I cannot be bothered—there will be mischeif Sir if I am in the least troubled depend upon it—You know all about Miss Allen—You know whether or not she is my cousin—and Mr Montmorency says you did meet her this morning—It could be to no good Percy for I have a deal of black blood, though I will not as I repeat threaten any one, and I could bear no interference with any arrangements of mine!—Then besides all that—all we have talked about—"

"Nay Thurston" remarked Percy "I have not talked at all—I have not the most distant idea of the goal which you would gain—I only know that we are delaying our sport incommoding our friends and, if the truth must bespoken, making cursed fools of ourselves."

Mr Thurston on hearing the calm and rather supercilious voice of Mr Percy seemed to suffer a mental change similar to what a wet blanket might physically produce if wrapped round a fevered body. He leaned on his gun and holding out his hand rather awkwardly replied

"I meant nothing wrong—nothing I assure you—I only wanted to know—that is I do know Mr Montmorency is a—"

"A Scoundrel" said Percy, finishing the sentence as without accepting Thurstons proffered hand he turned with hasty steps to rejoin his still hastier companions.

Mr Thurston followed with a look so sweet that O' Connor declared he had swallowed vitriolic acid instead of porter and Quamina swore he never had a blacker bargain from Camaroons or Congo rivers. Montmorency had long been joking with the Keepers who evidently marked him down as a delightful fellow and Mr Robert King had for an equal space of time been venting the indignation of outraged virtue upon the boys and grooms who held charge of the baskets. Now however—the two magnates having returned without black eyes or bloody noses and apparently on terms of friendship, however wide their hearts might be assunder—though one might be conscious of his mastership over and exulting in his powers to torture a being bound by this worlds laws to him in the old Hall far below them—and the other—two days since,

"Vacant hand and heart and eye"

now feeling a lawless abandonment of self to the white cheek and the melancholy eyes which from habitual discharge of a routine of duties hardly ever changed however much the heart might throb or the soul might sicken—Now, the procession felt at liberty to move, and with the wild moors before them the hopes of sport around them —the possession of sound health among them—for even old King was undecayed—why did they not feel truly happy?

Those whose lives lie within the walls of their library little know what has formed the existence of the men who have given them their treasures and those who know no feelings beyond domestic duties cannot divine the thoughts that cross strong but unbridled minds without a home to flee to or long lost to thoughts of home.

Among the gentlemen who formed this army against the 'Moors' who had a real home? Mr Montmorency had not—whose wife lay under the huge roof of Cologne Cathedral dead after a few years of sufferance under himself and a few months of the outbreak and indulgence of long felt and late enjoyed love of the man who 'left her alone to die'—That Man—Mr Percy had not—who besides such thorns in his flesh—such pinches as the old man Adam gave Christians— knew that cold earth embraced the little lady who never thought but for him— Nor had Mr O' Connor who felt bitterly that his rents as soon as due must be received not by his own itching fingers but by the widely expanding palm of Mr Jeremiah Simpson— Nor had the said Simpson whose nerves were troubled respecting the value of certain American and Spanish mortgages held from Mr Quamina Nor had Quamina whose soul longed by another venture on the now hazardous middle passage to gain enough to clear himself from Jeremiahs talons—Nor had Gordon who felt that his fate and fortune spun round with a teetotum—that Red and Black gave the colours to his chamelion destiny—Nor had probably any one of the fry of Servants Keepers watchers and drivers—for

"Each have their sufferings all are men
Condemned alike to groan
The feeling for anothers pain
The unfeeling for his own."

However a wide expanse of breezy highland heathers with the sun of the 'twelfth' tipping thro purple bloom and where broad breasts face a healthy breeze and Britains peculiar birds surrender their lives at every shot—was no place for remembering by past sorrows or participating in the feelings of the bard of Olney, and when at noontide the diverging groups of sportsman and attendants met at a lonely spring whose diamond water gushed up through deep green mosses in a dell of knee deep heather under a semicircle of whinstone rock they seemed all engrossed in the display of their bags or in excusing a want of display. Thurston from his knowledge of the ground and power over the underlings seemed to produce two or three brace more than any of his guests—O' Connor and Quamina who had given themselves up to the sport regardless of every other consideration save a pull at the whiskey flask ranked second as victors Montmorency could afford to swagger over Simpson and Gordon but all rode triumphant over the acknowledged best shot in the party—Mr Percy.

"Well" exclaimed Mr O' Connor turning over Percys single Cock-bird which was minus a head from some access of fury on the part of the shooter— "Well Gentlemen—hand me the flask—I have lived through many troubles in my time but this is a regular extinguisher upon all! To think that I have nine brace to shew against half an one from the best gun between Derbyshire and Westmoreland is enough to make me fancy I can pay off my debts—I can tell why Simpson and Gordon have failed for they have had their hands in their purses instead of on their triggers, and as for Montmorency—He's been thinking of his next breif in a 'crius cori' case or an action for assault and battery. Then Thurston can do as he pleases because the fellows about us know that when he wishes a nod is as good as a wink to a blind horse—but Percy with half a bird—I say Quamina hand me over the flask—Well may we have more Percy's ere the days out and then thou and I Quashia may do a little business at our old profits of 500 per cent."

Mr Quamina replied—"He is head over ears O' Connor—He is indeed Arthur! I see it in his squint at us two! He has bagged his bird before he donned his jacket and Thurston had better take care of that"—

"Who—I? What are you saying?" exclaimed the Host furiously but Mr Quamina evidently astonished swallowed all reply in another pull at his flask and so Mr Thurston turned to Percy for either an answer or a quarrel but as the latter saw Montmorency watching with an eager eye the cloud no bigger than a mans hand which should presage storms to others and pass unnoticed over himself; and as he was not desirous of being the victim of his friends or his hosts revenge he tossed off his horn of mountain dew—threw his single headless bird to his old servant and bidding him take care to bring the poney and his own skin safe back to Darkwall he lost no time in good mornings or excuses but dashed back across the gulley and down the long cart rut which served as a path from the peat pits to the farm steads of a more civilized land

I cannot be expected to dissect Mr Percy's feelings or emotions during his rapid walk back to Darkwall as I believe he scarce left time to do so himself but with a scorn of his morning employment a distaste toward his mornings companions and a revulsion of thoughts which made the whole twelfth a day of black chalks he sprung over the first style and strode over the first causeways through the twenty acre pastures of green land stolen from heather and made part and parcel of Darkwall farm

Percy did not make any halt in his intrusion so soon and so unexpectedly upon the quietude of a Hall which expected domestic slumber till evening brought in such visitors as might be willing to turn night into day. He made his return known to the Lady of the mansion and was received by her in the breakfast room

"I have returned so soon" he said "because I felt my hand was not in for sport and among men over whom I am accustomed to crow I do not like [to] appear second best so you as are aware that fruitless rest is better than fruitless labour I have returned to find in your mansion the ancient works of man which I can look at while seated on a sopha instead of the ancient works of nature which take so many miles of bog trotting to enjoy. How many hours of rest shall I have ere my sad crew return?"

"Thurston did not mention any certain time for the return of your party but I expected no one before six."

While Mrs Thurston spoke and during the first moments of her meeting with the unexpectedly arrived guest no servant about the establishment could have been so dull as not to percieve the embarrasment of their usually calm and sweet tempered Mistress—The eye which usually had a dove like glance for all—the voice which had a gentle tone and the steps which were so quiet now changed into a phase of irritation in manner—trouble in the eyes and hesitation both in voice and step—but a ready Key might have been given to these changes had the observers been aware of the risks she was running from an innocent breach of promises given to her furious husband and meant to be kept as faithfully as made, and the revulsion of all hospitable or lady-like feeling should she keep to the letter of her promise as well as the still small voice scarce daring to whisper amid conflicting winds which told a womans and a ladys heart that a visitor was sheltered under her roof whose mind possessd some mettle more attractive than ebullitions of sour reproach—whose feelings had a wider higher and deeper range than what would be exersised in attempts to ruin others or onse self—whose person likewise gave animated instead of cloudy looks gentle flexibility of tone instead of bilious snappishness—Eyes of mobile imaginativeness instead of bull-like suspicion—lips of winning sweetness instead of acerb ill temper, that she might now in fact have hoped for one happy afternoon after so many blank or blotted ones but for the grim threatning scowl which from neighbouring moors frowned upon her companionship the thunder shadows of resentment and revenge.

Percy took his station at a window which faced the moors and after a long look at moving clouds which from chrysalis like mists had condensed into an emphemeral life of sunny joy and on moors whose clearly defined outlines while they spoke to sportsmen of "the battle and the breeze," left his mind 'scaped from scenes of havoc which would make "e'en moorcocks weep" to recurr to former times and like the dove "to flee away and be at rest"

"One would think" he remarked without noticing the embarrassment in the manner of his hostess—"that these melancholy wastes rose above the warm atmosphere of pleasure and beyond the mild influences of sympathy but unless among the dull brick built streets and foggy air and filthy pavement of a town view, one seldom can see a natural prospect of which we can say truthfully "it is stark naught" I once sat not far from Scarboro' under a black wet semicircle of rock with no objects in sight except sand and star fish for a few yards in front and the tidal waves framed in the dark rocks of my cove which ended in a grey background of sea stretching parallel to a milky sky. Now one might ask where lay the charm that could keep me half an hour biting my cane and like the laird on his 'louping on stane' 'looking frae' me when if the prospect did embrace the three great objects of nature Heaven Earth and Ocean they would all have been seen to better advantage on the walls of the National Gallery or in the pages of a young ladies scrap book, and besides did not the ever changing tide of human life on the promenade offer a wider scope for reflection than the monotonous surges of the sea? Would not a railway cutting shew rock work in a more scientific as well as more shapely form than the shapeless and useless piles that girdled me? Would not even the little circular Museum hold forth at an easy distance more interesting specimens of geological and Zoological history than those afforded by the cornelian pebbles or limpet shells or starfish that sprawled among the narrow foreground of sand and sea weed? Very true Mrs Thurston—but neither science and the picturesque combined or any other compound known can produce at ones own will or that of another person the incommunicable emotions of an inward reflective joy."

"Joy is not the appropriate term for it I think Sir."

"How do you know that? I was aware of my mistake but I did not imagine a lady would discover it."

"Perhaps one who has been for years accustomed to see natural beauty only in grey walls and naked fields and barren moors may—although a woman— have attained to some expertness in extracting from them what they have to give of subdued emotion or pleasurable calm. The owner of Chatsworth must not fancy he alone has a delight in Flora because he owns a five hundred feet Conservatory. The heath bloom or the daisy or the foxglove with "its silent peal of bells" may give a thrill of pleasure to the walker through rushy fields and over boggy moors which could not have been exceeded by Schomburgh himself when he first saw the immense Victoria flower gleaming among the reeds of the Essequibo"

"You speak justly—but—I know not how it is—I do not like to hear women speak thus as it appears that they have to fall back on indefinable musings for a refuge from palpable care. Let such rescources be left to a fellow like myself as I should be as cloud capped as ever was Boulshill yonder if I thought that a wife of mine were like a bee sucking comfort from wild flowers on the ridge of his heathy brow! But I suppose we must all get happiness where we can and if it escapes our pursuit we must not repine. Were we born into this world for happiness or is joy the puzzling and contradictory exception to the routine engagements of life and sorrow the Egyptian task work which binds us to our long life-day's work of toil?

"We have guides Sir in even the most intricate journey and of these Duty is one very safe if sometimes unpleasing. Rectitude of conduct points out the straightest road from this to the other world and hope if healthy will help one over ordinary obstacles and if feverish it will do us more harm than what might be caused by the common excitement of wine. Resignation I would recommend as a faster friend than either for it neither craves for hope or fears despair."

Mr Percy did not immediately reply to Mrs Thurstons words but he took his seat on the sopha leaned his head on his hand and surveyed the furniture of the room with eyes that might have been mistaken for those of an Auctioneer or Upholsterer had not their matter of fact inquisitiveness been contradicted and relieved by the peculiar smile of his mobile lips. Mrs Thurston was already seated at her little work table and examined her embroidery frame with an attention which might have been as much mistaken as his own—for the patience with which she proceeded in her work partook of the commonplace character of—not perhaps an Upholsterer—but a Power loom weaver—Still the dark eye lashes, bent ever downwards, seemed sometimes moist; and she never once looked at his face whose gaze (though with no difference in expression from that which examined her footstool) was so often bent on hers. One of those pauses in which thought seems struggling among the meshes of a net which it has not the power to break and wherein a few minutes of silence send ones mind flying over a score of years occurred to give additional abstraction to both the lady's and the gentlemans countenance, till Mr Percy broke the ice by soliloquizing—

"What a fool they will think me to escape so soon and with half a brace from the sports of so sweet a twelfth of August! Had I brought down a bag crammed with birds flesh and feathers—had I been able to boast of dozens instead of units I had been a hero but now—reclining at noon in Thurstons parlour while my companions are roaming ten thousand acres of heather is really a virtual resignment of my sportsmans crown—Well—when I have nothing else to think of or when I want to drive off all thought I can be as sharp a shot and as stalwart a walker as any one but when I am out o' the vein I will not brag of performances worthy of being registered in any column of Bells Life in London. What have I returned for? My head can not tell me and I wonder if my heart could give me my reason."

"Perhaps your caprice might—for people generally give you credit for the possession of that uncertain quality."

Mr Percy turned his face towards his hostess as he half reclined on the cushions and said rather growlingly

"Do people in general fancy me like an actor or an Opera dancer and do you imagine that my return hither was because I liked whin-rocks built into a wall better than whin rocks scattered over a moor? That I preferred my host's servants to my host's guests? That I was attacked by a 'male green sickness' and loved chalk better than cheese? No I believe you to be so far advanced in sense and so well able to appreciate motives or divine intentions as to feel that I returned because a couple of hours spent with yourself would appear one hour and three quarters shorter in the registered revolution of this sun than the same time spent among the pursuits I travelled hither to take part in—because I hoped to find in you the gaslight which in a Theatre or ballroom apologises for the

"gay beams of lightsome day"

You are aware that being a forlorn widower my daylight has winked its wearied eye and dreams or fancies only can restore in the present and future night those alleviations to trouble which fate and fortune have carried far off and far away. Should I very hastily ride back at the risk of a horses knees or walk back at the risk of my own to see Mr O' Connor or Mr Quamina discuss a couple of bottles before luncheon—to calculate the value of the estates yet to be or just having been mortgaged by them with Simpson and Gordon—to try with Hector which of the two could look most treacherous or with Thurston which could look most sour? No—no—I returned as if to a shadow of my ancient returning during years wherein I could doff my shooting dress and find a face to welcome me milder than that of a man though that man might be a friend—You are looking confused and serious but you need not do so as I must speak what I feel and what I feel is not in want of a cloak"—

"Indeed Sir I was only about to rise to ring the bell as I am sure you must need refreshment and probably Miss Allen, my husband's cousin, who will soon arrive from her walk will join you—I believe she did not expect you here though—any more than myself."

"Madam—mark me—Do you not think it strange in a person to invite another to dinner and set before him a service of plate but forget all the viands— Then will it not be strange in yourself to welcome me hither and refuse the only pleasure that could make me feel pleased? I see you are about to retire but as my time in this house must be short why try to make that time uncomfortable? Why try to afflict with midnight frost mental leaves that only want for due development an hour or so of morning dew and sunny balm? Do not allow anxiety to spoil your eyes as I see it is doing whenever I notice you to look at the carriage road or listen to the door bell—You have had havoc enough played with your marble cheeks ere now without seeking for any further bleaching and though I heed little who enters here I must if you look so sad much longer be vividly reminded of the different looks with which eyes now closed for ever expected and watched for my own returns. Oh it is true that a soul too lovely for the tempests of this wretched life—too blessed to have a long abidence here may still not die but slumber—and forgetting its own decaying body wake after a few years of repose in the shelter of a corporeal shrine as congenial and as fair. Do not leave the room—I was only permitting a hasty temper to indulge in expectations which can never be fulfilled and I will not be frowned upon if I own that THY womanly gentleness has tamed a heart which sorrow was making sadly too wild.

"I think I see Miss Allen coming up the walk and so you will soon have more cheerful company than any I can give."

"I do not desire cheerfulness" said Mr Percy rising and pacing rapidly through the apartment—"I want some thing of more value—some thing which will not leave me with a joke or a smile—I want—Why before Miss Allen enters I want Thy hand in proof that I have not angered Thee, or at least in acknowledgement that with thee reproof of an offence may be mingled with pardon for the offender—Come, as my hostess thy hand must be placed in mine—or I have no alternative save to ride off directly or open out a budget of quarrels—God bless the fingers which can by one touch give a whole days life to me—"

So Mr Percy spoke with some haste and much earnestness as he clasped Mrs Thurstons hand while she was passing—and standing over her with a look of mingled love and sorrow besought by such a glance pardon from her brow and sympathy from her eyes—but well for her equanimity of temper and in full accordance with the gentlemans calculations it happened that ere Mrs Thurston could say a sentence or retire a step the door was opened to admit Miss Louisa Allen on her arrival from her solitary mornings walk.

Miss Allen looked highly flushed and breathed very rapidly but that might have been owing to her hurried return—She did not speak to Mrs Thurston—express[ed] her astonishment in a few syllables at Mr Percys desertion of his companions and then threw aside with some impatience the incumbrances of bonnet and mantle.

Mr Percy looked at her with an expression of risibility on his countenance and told her that of the two she seemed more like one who had followed the sports of that morning than himself, for he felt as cool as a cucumber while her cheeks were in a July glow. However only replying that if he felt like a cucumber she felt like a water melon Miss Allen went to the window and Percys laughing eye could mark the entering sunlight glisten on a cheek wet with a few tears not of sensibility to the lovely wilds before her but of that most reckless of all feelings a womans bad temper. He turned from that face to another expressing an equally true picture of a woman but as it was now again bent over the embroidery frame how different seemed the effect of the view & the parks of Windsor and the silver Thames beheld from Richmond hill could not be less like the great Glen beheld from Ben Nevis than was the sweet resignation which compassionated anothers ruffled temper from the rebellious look which nursed and lived on revenge for all causes of disquiet that might thwart its will.

"How pleasant" he remarked seating himself on the sopha and talking at Miss Allen if not to her. "How much milder the feelings produced by a retirement into a primitive district from the false fitful fever of a life in town— Had I been now in the Metropolis and were it now before the prorogation I should have been obliged to dress and paint my soul in all manner of false colours to meet and mix with souls which could no more mingle with mine than oil could with water—To pass compliments with women whose dead corpses would no more affect my real feelings than their living charms—to keep terms of friendship with men who would cause me much more pleasure by a communication with them through my boot toes instead of the tips of my fingers—Here now I find nature in its unsophisticated state—Hills that laugh to scorn the ploughshare a park that absolutely gives a 'guffaw' to Sir Henry Stewart of Allanston—a room that exersises[sic] as much decorum in its admission of sunlight from Heaven as did the court under whose auspices it was built in the encouragement of sunlight from eyes—Aye and I suspect more for Queen Bess could see a trim leg among her nobles at a score of yards distance and Mrs Thurston cannot see her needle at an inch from her eye. Miss Allen alone has telescopic power of vision for she looks earnestly for planets or constellations through a heaven wherein I can only see hot autumnal vapours and a single mackarel cloud."

"Perhaps" answered the lady with a rather unsuccessful attempt at cheerfulness—"My cloud may afford a more substantial prospect than words which disguise or don't know their meaning."

"Perhaps a flitch of Bacon—nay a glass of flummery may be more substantial than "Angels ever bright and fair." The first is substance the last sound—but not the less worthy of remembrance when coupled with the alliance of a thrilling voice and jet black eyes."

The reference to Handels song evidently aided in temporarily soothing the little vixen like person at the window who seemed to have a dream of W——— Cathedral and of an Organist pushed from his seat to make way for the touch of fingers inspired as much by a syrens voice as by the organs roll, and of one who beheld as he touched the Keys not the portly and comely presence of Mr George Frederic Handel but the sylph like figure of one whom she could at any hour behold in the glass with raven locks as Symmons has it

"like midnight loosed at noon"

So she turned more animatedly from her long look at Boulshill and for the first time since her entrance into the room vouchsafed a smile—Perhaps Percy noticed that it was rather one of triumph at momentary success over a fancied rival than at disinterested love of his praise, so he changed his varying features till their powers seemed wreaked on the beads that were gradually forming the roses and tulips of Mrs Thurstons work, and then Miss Allen rousing from silenc[e]d irritability saying—

"You may court the sunshine but as the day grows so sultry I will seek shade—I don't think I shall walk—love—before luncheon," She departed leaving behind her the embarrasment produced by the departure of one much displeased from a company wherein no one wished to cause displeasure—and yet I fear the absence of so bright a planet did not give a more midnight hue to the sky which in Mr Percys eyes did sem to contain some scarce explored or erratic star while in those of his hostess it held—if her sad cheek could tell anything— no light whatever—save the ignus fatuus of decay which lights up the enamel remnants of time past or the half despair and half hope which through present frosty skies of winter affords a fitful Aurora borealis to mock the sunshine of Youths summer in the Greenland heavens of time to come. Mrs Thurston looked as if desirous of following her lady guest but a scowling eye pursued her through a meandering search among sideboards for skeins of silk wherein every tack was doorwards till she could feign no longer but placidly returned to her seat and reassumed the hostesses benignness

"Now then" remarked Percy "Summer will have its thunderstorms and noe has just past by with but one peal—I ought to be thankful; for judging from my fair foes eyes a commmon flash of lightning would be nothing to the effect educible from their volcanic fire. Why is it that slender frames enclose such daring spirits while a creature like myself of six feet two can only baa like a new cast lamb?"

The very handsome mouth of Mr Percy as he uttered the last sentence curled into a positively ugly sneer and moved for once a smile on the rather too pallid lips of the lady who listened to him—She replied without looking up from her work

"Fits of temper among theose of our sex seem rational compared with those among yours—If we feel aggrieved past endurance we can at least leave the room whereas you seem disposed to stay and covertly vex persons whom the rules of society forbid you openly to insult"

"And do you apply so severe a censure as your words would imply, to me? Do you think I have returned from an aimless and tiresome journey so soon to spend the time which should have been occupied in killing Moorgame in plaguing women? Two there are of your sex to whom I have spoken this morning and one I am sure I have no wish to irritate or displease—the other now seated opposite to me must retire into her own heart to answer the enquiry does she dislike me more or less than the dozens or scores of country boors that alone have awaked her silver voice since the day she left Euston Square Station?—She knows God has not blighted me with the thunderbolt of personal deformity or the Typhoon of repulsive manners—She must feel that what bad passions and tempers I have are caged up or rioting in a wildernesses far apart from her sylvan shades—That I have no wish to exert my superior bodily strength save to preserve her from harm or my more impetuous temper save to infuse vigour into her mildness—That I forget the black daemons of melancholy partly because her aspect scares them and partly because my anxiety for her comfort subdues them—That indeed I am here just now because God's goodness has given to me for a short time a daily drop of 'elixir vitae' in my cup of restless misery—A sweet remembrance—my girl—of thoughts which must be innocent because they lie wholly in the grave and are only called forth again in this room as among the snows of December you would open the phial which held the essence of Julys rose. You must not rise I—once more repeat—for luncheon is I suppose nearly ready and neither I or yourself—I mean yourself or I would partake of it with more relish from knowing that anger or insult or false modesty or conventional manners had separated our tables or our hearts.Look at this Old Hall Maria Thurston—is it a hypocrite? Look at that mirror—does it tell lies? Look at what that mirror reflects—Is it an image qualified to shine only in a London crowd of fashionables or over the benches of a Methodist conventicle? You KNOW you are a lady and that a man if worthy of the name can neither dislike or even feel indifferent to you. You know that you are a neglected lady and that I know you are so. You know too that I would lose lifes blood to drive injury from you and sacrifice its comforts to give you pleasure and if you know so much my girl you likewise know that I am not returned hither to change for you this balmy twelfth of August into a weeping twelfth of April, but to indulge a selfish desire for happiness in conversation with you and to exersise a most unselfish feeling in contributing to the ease of the gentle heart which beats within that corset and cheering the hours of a lady who too often I fear has to spend them alone. Cannot I have some stores of knowledge from which to furnish an hours innocent amusement when while her bosom has only brooded dovelike over home scenes my wandering wings have expanded like those of the stormy peteril over lifes ocean through every clime and climate—every grief and joy."

"Yes Sir I know well your mind has among its stores of wealth much that is valuable and that any one might feel happy in your society if that mind chose to let others partake of its stores"

"Let others partake! No not all others But oh thine own dear self should and gladly too! What is that obscurely seen but most overwhelming incubus which forbids me—weighs me down when I dare dream of a pleasure so great as this afternoon spent apart from the world and seated by thy side—yet making what I have known of the world and indeed my whole store of thought, subservient to thy pleasure who while nursed in quiet and comfort might thus explore the ocean of humanity without being buffeted by its storms?"

"You have from indulgence been accustomed Sir to feel too impatient when your days do not pass in unclouded sunshine—many pleasures one might hope for on awaking in the morning but so few are realized during the day that I accustom myself to receive each visitation of joy as a boon—not as a right or even a thing to be expected and this feeling constantly cultivated allows me to go through my duties and bear any mortifications with such calmness as makes mind and body able to drink the cup of sorrow without a wry face and feel no intoxication from the cup of joy"

"Then is it Gods will and according to a just disposal of events that I should now return to disliked or uncongenial companions and leave you hugging your chain and like an Indian devotee proud to show that you can take your nap on a bed of ten penny nails or like a pugilist that you can smile after a sledge hammer hit on your teeth? Answer me—would it be well—would it accord with your ideas of justice should two persons resolve to do all they could to prevent mutual friendship and produce mutual pain?"

"No Sir—I believe our object ought to be the promotion of friendship and alleviation of pain."

"To both ones own self and to all others?"

"Yes—as I would not reccommend suicide most certainly to ones self— but even before oneself to others because if every one in this world thought first of his neighbour and last of himself we should eventually be sure of happiness. Do not you see that for one grain of pleasure sacrificed every point of the compass would return you a hundred fold?"

"And You—or myself are to don the pasteboard helmet of the Spanish hero and sally forth with the idea of sacrificing our happiness to the good of our fellow creatures, are we? No, no. It is enough that I wish to live for one being beside[s] myself and not for one thousand millions. I wish by word and deed to comfort one whom I love and I only ask as a reward that she should not wholly dislike me."

Mr Percy had now entered upon one of his usual fit[s] of restless walking through an apartment which always attacked him when much excited and while obliged to hide feelings which inborn nature and constant indulgence through life impelled him to display. He would not so much as look at the fair face bending over a mechanical employment lest it should not precisely tally with his notion of the emotions he fancied it ought to feel and lest he should forget what was due to the gentleman under whose roof he was staying and by one wild outbreak of passion throw himself open to three alternatives of misery. The ruin of a Lady whom his very soul did really love just then—the risk of a bullet through his bosom from the pistol of the dark bilious faced person under whose roof he abode, and, worst of all, denial of Love—of sympathy—of sorrow for himself and dearly purchased knowledge of coldness and dislike from an answer to the half dozen sentences which were tingling on his tongue and to which the consciousness of their importance alone prevented him giving utterance. He dreaded every movement made by Mrs Thurston lest it should announce her departure from the room. He felt jealous of every change on her mild thoughtful face lest it should herald some stern avowal of feelings if toward himself, still severed by duty and that last idea so gained upon his mind that he broke the silence of the room by one abrupt question.

"Now Maria Thurston—I must be here for days or weeks and I must not during that time be laid on St Lawrences gridiron—So I ask you once and for all—will you—by preserving your thoroughly womanlike character and by allowing me to rest upon its feminine sweetness my masculine roughness—let my stay here be passable to my mind or will you shun me and make me conscious of the truth of that hideous saying that women care not for any man but live for the gratification of a vanity whose shrine is their looking glass or the hecatomb of real manly hearts that have burst under their whims and which will send up a fragrance when consuming on the altar of that Nova Zembla deity a bloodless woman proud to keep a real man in pain."

"But Sir you have been married yourself and I should not intrude on your feelings perhaps by asking you whether or not your own lady assumed the semblance of a Nova Zembla deity Did she only care for you as the means whereby she could gratify her vanity—did she never feel toward her husband as if pain to him would be double pain to herself?"

"Maria Thurston—You distress me—I have lost the sole charm of a fevered and broken life and I would willingly and innocently fill up the dreadful chasm that lies between the grave of her whom I did possess and the goal whose laurels must sooth the worry of my forthcoming life. What if that goal be yourself? Why should you shrink from intercommunion with myself whose every sinew would rouse to save your little finger from harm—Who besides me would make his life a secondary consideration to yours? Who besides me would foresake mans idol pleasure to worship what is too often womans idol pain—Who would, though you call him indulged, bear the pains of a prison to see you enjoy the pleasures of a palace.

You know what I mean Maria—You know what I have lost and what I would gain. Tell me—do you think that one who has for years been accustomed to repose a worried and wearied head on a warm and devoted bosom—now that the bosom is given over to corruption and that he is forced to feel jealous of worms—do you think that he no longer wants such a repose and while clouds are gathering and years closing round him he feels no wish for a ressurection of his buried joy? When I leave Darkwall and return to Percy Hall shall I not feel a sad vacancy when my lonely evenings after dinner are spent in studies where a weary head misses sadly the little hand that used to stroke its hair or the soft lap that used to ease its aching—where my little girl alone will give all that childhood can of affection but where I shall leave among northern clouds and heather the polar star of love—Oh do not start Maria Thurston for you too will think of me when I am gone—You will know too well what place you fill now—What place I would have you to fill to feel indifferent to Alexander

Percy. Hours which did fate permit it—might be spent in a recalled paradise by my fireside will perforce contrast themselves with hours of neglect present to your heart and senses here. I am sure that ere the winds of winter blow the sleet against these windows you will have dropped some tears over the doom which denies to Maria Thurston the place of Mary Percy!"

"Sir—Sir—you must restrain this speech—I cannot bear it and beg you as a gentleman to spare me."

"Must I not rather Maria—beg you to spare me? She whose heart is resigned to suffering has little to fear but his heart who feels that there is no medium between agony and enjoyment has every thing to dread especially if former time reappears like a ghost in the unattainable yet tantalizing prospects of the present time. Where shall we each be a year hence Maria? Were shall we be to night? Why I—if asleep at all—shall lie dreaming of ideas that

"Remind me of departed times—

Departed—never to return"

and you I am sure will be compelled to fancy that your uncherished cheek might be better nurtured than by comforts which stern crowns and hard usage could give you—Ah—You know not and till you shall have been tried you cannot know the yearnings of a mans heart left alone toward the heart of a woman whom he would wish to be part and parcel with himself.

"Oh Sir" exclaimed Mrs Thurston earnestly and with a face suddenly overmastered by pain—"Do not try to make me miserable —I have my sorrows and I have hitherto born them patiently. It can do no one good to remind me of lifes path mistaken or of pleasure to which it is impossible to attain"

"Then" answered Mr Percy while his expressive features beamed with serpent guile only rendered more dangerous from the intermixture of real anxiety—"Does Maria Thurston mean to enact a Suttee? Does she wish to immolate herself on the pile raised for a husband who never existed must she feel bound for ever to a master whom she scarce knows save by his tyranny and repulse the heartfelt sympathy of a friend?"

"A friend Sir! Do you not mock me by your use of the word?"

"I do. Maria, if the drowning man clings to a swimmer or a plank for salvation—if one who has had no peace in this life tries to drive despair from his death bed by his hopes of heaven. But I do not if my soul chooses thee as successor to a throne long vacant and a sceptre which no hand save thine can sway—Would that I could make thee believe me! Thou must know that I cannot pass a future existence on the mere memory of love—That one so young as I am will require to support his soul through a probably protracted life some encouragement better than a look backward on a sunny path while clouds and tempests brood over his forward road. But I will not argue—Thou lovest me and thou knowest that thou lovest me—Stop—do not answer or I shall push thee into perjury by asking at once "Dost thou hate me?" and as thy answer would certainly be "Yes" thou wouldest be utterly forsworn. Can I not read thy thoughts on thy pillow to night? and canst thou not read my own? Yes—yes— And if thyself and myself were kneeling together at the parsons altar thou wouldst waste but few moments of hesitation ere saying—however inaudibly with Addison and Haydn

"Lo my Shepherd is divine
How shall I want while he is mine"

The strange character which both adorned and cursed the speaker was exemplified in his last sentence for while absorbed in a subject which engrossed every mental and personal feeling he waywardly sported with a sneering allusion to a few lines of verse and a beautiful snatch of pastoral music. which would have given his eyes the aspect of an angels had he been forced to take his seat at an organ or piano. But here—reclined on a sopha in this quiet ancient apartment and in the company of one who whatever she suffered would never give pain—He let his looks stray scenting the track of pleasure and his mind run hydrophobically biting at those whom his calmer feelings would lead him to cherish.

The morning sunlight shone through the window of a chamber in the Hotel, upon a head of curly auburn hair, a sad, pale face, and quivering lips laid on a restless pillow and shewing every feature in sickly guise save the wicked blue eyes that—to any one who knew their owner—augered some new ray of mischeivous caprice breaking through the clouds of sickness. Their owner, after a gentle sigh or two rung the bell and the chamber maid appeared.

"Fanny" said Percy "Whether my old groom be dead or alive—drunk or sober—send him to me forthwith."

"Yes Sir—He has been up all night Sir, with some north country jobbers—They've been very noisy Sir."

"And, Fanny, bring me a tumbler of Hollands with a dash of water in it, and—stop—I have something to say to you—Take a sovereign out of my waistcoat pocket—With ten shillings purchase mob caps, and with the other ten procure yourself a quantity of tracts which you can distribute about the house during the fair and by all means lay one on each tray that the waiters may bring in to company, as well as on every bed in the house."

"There are some pretty songs Sir in one of the stalls"

"Oh **** my—I mean Religious tracts my girl! Those printed at the Wesleyan Repository in London."

Fanny looked at her sovereign as if destining it for another voyage than the one marked in her chart

"And, Fanny, take down those curls, and comb your hair parted in front—come here and I will shew you the way."

Saying "Oh no Sir I can do it myself" Fanny departed on her errand, rather indignant that her favourite ornaments should be censured, and wholly puzzled to know what that strange wild gentleman meant this morning.

She shortly returned with the morning draught required, and along with her stumbled in the patriarchal form of old Robert, much afflicted with "all overishness" and modelling his face into the expression of a Lord Eldon pronouncing judgement on a chancery suit of a century in duration and a plum in value.

"Well—you doubly hanged dog! Drunk as an owl I see! What have you been doing all night?"

"Searching after me truth Maister." ë

"I have heard Truth was to be found at the bottom of a well, but I did not know it was a well of rum and water—But however—Bob, I have turned over a new leaf—I will neither Swear, *****, drink, gamble, rob, or commit manslaughter again—**** me if I will!"

"Thank Him that Saves! O Maister yaw're in a fearful gooid way!" and the old Saint clasping his hands together uttered a rapturous groan.

"Are you sober enough Bob to rattle through a healing prayer for me? Anything that has enough grace in it will come in nicely—Stay, Fanny, give me the tumbler—and halt Bob—have you never such an article as a Hymn book about you?"

"Aw've getten the varry best" replied Robert, lugging out an old black greasy volume—"Its the Selection used amang the Primitive Methodists—commomly termed Ranters—Owd John Wesla's nought to it—It warms folk till the divil could'nt tak' 'em."

"**** it! That's the true Nightingale! But Fanny my girl fetch me another glass—and then we'll silence the Angels. Bob—This life will never do— I have a Soul to be saved—"

"Sure—sure Maister"

"And—**** me if I won't save it'"

"The Lord be praised—Yaw're in a gooid way Maister!"

"Well then—pitch the Key note—thats it—I'll take the tenor—

"Will you go to Glory with me &c &c"

The effect of the ensuing duet was most farcical were it not blasphemous. The beautiful tenor of Mr Percy united in all possible earnestness with a voice that tortured ones ears like that of a mad Jack ass, and, as is usual with the sect from whose book the words were selected, to a tune which might be fitly accompanied by the dance of a 'hen on a het girdle[sic]'.

The poor young chambermaid stood sincerely pitying 'the nice mad gentleman' but utterly unable to repress a feminine titter. But a much deeper and more masculine chuckle could be heard ere the door opened to introduce Hector Matthias Mireabeau Montmorency, Esqre—whose perfect knowledge of his friends character had made him—on hearing from his bedroom the melodious twang—arise, don his garments, and straight proceed to perfect the work of godliness—

"Now then my heroes!" thundered the Barrister "Which is to fly fastest toward Heaven—Master or man? You want a good bass and as I flatter myself I possess such an article, while I am sure, from your chambermaids pretty mouth she has a sweet treble—we'll make up four parts, and walk up faster than Enoch or Elijah—I am a Calvinist and believe Jerry and Quashia and O' Connor and Gordon were predestined to the fire grate so I wont call them in to join us."

"Oh, but Hector, I am not a Calvinist I am as good a Wesleyan as was ever hatched—and I insist that all shall be saved—Storming heavens gate[s] is the duty of a Christian soldier—I am a new born child Hector —Fanny just reach me the tumbler—and I'll be—" Here the speakers voice was drowned by a violent fit of coughing in consequence of too strong a draught of the spirits—at last he gained his breath to ask—

"Fanny—have they never a room in the house into which one could put a few forms and a pulpit during the fair time?"

"Yes Sir—Master has a large room up stairs, but the players are using it now"

"The players be damned—stop. **** me if I will swear again—I'll rent it and fit up a pulpit by G—d."

"The loard be praised said Robert, who was steadying himself against the bed post—and "Amen" groaned Hector—who was taking the sweetest pinch of snuff he had ever enjoyed. The groom, by virtue of his superior age and the advanced state of his religious experience thought proper to break in on the conversation of his Master and the Barrister by recommending that they should go to prayer.

"And donnot pray like frightened folk" said Bob "pray wi' a real thundering roar—pray till ye're legs kick aat like a stallion's—There's nought but muckment in ye're church prayers—Aw wad not dry my nose wi' 'em! If Heaven's grace will not come yaw mun mak' it come!"

I shall not give the report of Mr Robert Patrick King's prayer as though too true to nature, and to what I have often heard in Yorkshire and Lancashire—it would be very justly pronounced impious by all not intimately aquainted with the lengths to which a brutal character and an impudent hypocrisy like that which the excellent groom possessed, can carry the most notorious scoundrels through all the deliria of 'revivals' and 'experiences'.

Mr Percy lay, ejaculating between the pauses of his spiritual physician—such sentences as "Holy Melchizedec, Nebuchadnezzar and Batholomew look down upon us!" "Belshazzar, Jeroboam and Abihu, save us!" and when Hector remarked mildly "My Lad such invocations are neither Jew or Gentile—Catholic or protestant" He replied "Well I mean all for the best—Sweet Saint Bathsheba—dear Jezebel—divine Herodias have mercy on us!"—There Mr King fairly stopped in horror and amazement—

"Oh Loard! Maister—yaw're noan calling on them whores are ye? —Nay naw aw mun strip me coil to me wark and link at it in me shirt sleeves!"

"Well Bob it is not a sin to pray to Angels then—so—Merciful Moloch—blessed Belial—beneficent Beelzebub do have—"

"Stop Maister—They war angels once, but they've fallen like cracked pots, or a brocken kneed horse—Yaw mun look aboon Maister; same as aw do!"

The morning service had not proceeded much further, and Hector was just preparing to administer pedestrian admonition to the hinder man of the kneeling groom, when in burst Simpson Quamina and O' Connor—

"By Gom!" thundered Jeremiah in his deepest voice "Are we going to have a case of Delirium tremens here? By Gom—rise you fool"

"This" remarked Arthur "This is just the practical part of what I went through after my famous Fortnight where in I killed young Phillpot—He went off with a red hot poker in his bowels one Friday, after his thirty ninth tumbler—I had three Methodist missionaries at Kingston to pray for me that week—and it was all owing to new rum. It could be nothing else, for if it had been real old Jamaica he would have yet been sweet as a daisy."

"Well" said Quamina "You Christian dogs do pay dearly for your whistle—who ever heard any of the faithful ranting and raving thus?

Allah be praised—I am a Moslem skin and bone, and I'd be damned before I'd taste one drop of your infidel wine! Praised be the name of the prophet! I'm glad he knew nothing of Brandy and Whiskey! If He had done I doubt I should have found Houri's rather scarce hereafter!"

"Quashia Quamina" said Percy sternly "If you do not put off the old man I'll make you as much a cinder as you seem to be! That Bull baiting stake shall not have been standing so long in the towngate for nothing! Fanny my lass—tell the waiter to order—Coffee, Ham, Eggs—and Brandy for one—and lay a Bible beside the tray open at the Xth chapter of Nehemiah—you may as well also double it down at the Ist chapter of Ist Chronicles—I'll have prayers this morning or else I'll be—"I'll comment on Nehemiah from the 1st to the 27th verses—I'll let you know the word!"

All the bed chamber audience now left the room except the devout groom and the faithful friend, Hector, who said

"Now—Percy how long is this blasted foolery to continue—for I fancy you have other fish to fry?"

"Hector, if you do not leave this room and let me find you on my descent into the breakfast room, prone on your knees may you get ere night what you will be sure to get ere the Lords last day!"

Mr Montmorency shut the door, saying, ere he left that he hoped there was plenty of Hollands distributed at Love feasts, and Mr Percy with the aid of his devout groom and a snatch now and then from one of the songs of Zion managed to complete his morning toilette—which was not this morning the garb of a grouse shooting Squire—but very unexceptionable and clerical black. He sported a white cravat with a precise tie, and as his groom said on adjusting his masters crock coat—he "at last looked dacent and menseful—"

When the "Rev" Alexander Percy entered the breakfast room in his hotel he was greeted by the irrepressible laughter of his companions, but not all their mirth or raillery could disturb the rapt inspiration of his divine countenance. Addressing himself to the waiter, who, owing to confusion of mind consequent on the metamorphosis of the strange gentleman, was only prevented by Hector from misplacing everything. He said—

"Have you here any resident teachers of the Gospel?"

"No Sir—Yes Sir—Theres Mr Scarlet the Curate—a capital judge of horse flesh Sir—and the Rev Matthew Rasper—poor old Gentleman—he weighs 18st now and can scarce go to cover—but he loves to see a throw off. Boots will take you there Sir, any time. He has as good a drop of wine in his cellars Sir as we have—and the Dean says ours is not to be beaten at the Bishops—and I am sure the Dean is a judge Sir"

The company pricked up their ears at this intelligence—Quashia swore he loved the cloth for it was his own colour—O' Connor asked had Mr Rasper never a pretty daughter or so, for his soul warmed toward the family—but Mr Percy sternly ordered silence and continued—

"Waiter jest not on things pertaining to Salvation—Are there here any of the Lords labourers in the Wesleyan or Primitive Methodist vineyards"

"The Waiter looked at his napkin—settled his stock and timidly answered

"Lord Reynard has some gardeners Sir, but I believe they are not methodists, for the head gardener broke anothers head last week for selling off peaches—besides his lordship lives eight miles off Sir."

"Unrepentant Sinner—send for your Wesleyan preacher—and tell him to bring a brace of class leaders along with him"

As the waiter left the room scratching his head and sighing deeply Mr Percy took his place at the head of the table and intimated to the company that he should expect every man to off the moor and down at the Hotel by five in the afternoon, for the lord had work for them—For himself he should not touch a trigger as his vocation was to save souls.

"I always thought" said Hector who alone seemed thouroughly to comprehend his dear friends humour—"I always had an idea that the black coat carries it with the lasses over the red or green—Well I'll make one—and now you dogs when your luncheon is ready on the heather see if I don' t treat you to a grace as long as O' Connors face has become at the mention of it"

"Well" Sighed Arthur—turning to Quamina "There is nothing for it but to get drunk to day—trouble is pressing hard on us!"

"I am for a row and a fight in the fair this evening Arthur—nothing else will unburthen my mind."

"Gentlemen" said Percy—"You will do no such thing—The lord hath need of you. Hector I rely on you to follow out the good work."

As the Waiter, on reaching the preacher['s] door had said that the famous "RICH" gentleman staying at their house wished to see him my readers will not wonder that the saintly man knocked over his breakfast table—forgot the ham and eggs that were trembling under his ruthless knife, and in a whirl of calculations about the Chapel debt—quarterly subscriptions—Donations to a dozen different funds—visions of a new school such as should cut the national one to ribbons. The founders name "A. PERCY. ESQr"—on a vast marble tablet with the "Revd Simon Slugg Preacher of the Gospel" and all the Chapel trustees sheltering modestly under the aristocratic wing, beneath—that in such a state of unworldly extasy he broke both shins over the sheep pens and received martyrdom from three horse Jobbers whips ere he had roused up his two principal class leaders Messrs Apollos Fleshbotham, and Timothy Bottomley.

Those chosen vessels being rigid Teatotallers and knowing that when received gratis creature comforts were never refused by their beloved brother, were at first alarmed lest some hospitable brother or more probably sister, had tempted the lords servant over night—but when wiping his perspiring brow, the Rev Simon gasped out that the "RICH" gentleman at the Thurston Arms wanted them—they too caught a wild infection and each dashing his hat over his brows with the back run in front they burst through gathering the crowd of long and short horns—stopped not to rebuke the glaring lies which were bursting from each dealers lips, and soon made their appearance before the bar of the Thurtson Arms. Once only Bottomley asked Fleshbotham "Whats our Chapel debt?"

"£737=13s=6 3/4"

"Oh nonsense"—said Slugg "Say at once 1200—Its the lords work!"

Messrs Fleshbotham and Bottomley were beauties of the order combining that interesting union of darkness and pallor so assiduously cultivated by those that prefer the straight and narrow path. If their necks were not swanlike they yet stretched several inches above their carelessly tied white neckcloths and so far as stature may become a man, and flexibility be termed a constituent of grace, their lanky figures and loose jointed limbs proclaimed them to be model Apollos. Their Rev brother, though a few inches beneath the heroic standard, made amends by capacity of body for all he might be deficient in as to height and though his face looked like a pale "whangby" cheese, yet it was juicy enough to cause it to shine like the full moon through a fog.

Such as they were, the children of grace were admitted to the breakfast room, and saw first what made their fasting bowels yearn—a large table covered with the reliquae of a sportsmans morning meal—and next five very unevangelical 'professors' seated over "Fireballs" each consisting of a wine glass of brandy with the yolk of an egg dropped into it; but the object of their attraction stood before them on the hearth rug—a very tall divine looking saint, with eyes distorted almost to a squint—a mouth that changed its play each moment from wrapt solemnity to malicious drollery, and a pair of orange whiskers horribly out of harmony with the holy sable of his scrupulously neat attire.

As the trio kept each man his mouth open it followed that, physiologically considered, they could not speak—so Mr Percy began with a voice whose sonorous and noble tone gave them delightful anticipations of the effect of ensuing speeches in the Chapel—

"My Christian friends—Welcome in His name—come forward—Do your bodies need refreshment?"

"Why Sir, Why, no—That is we have hoped so much from an early exhibition of what He can do, that—in short Sir we thought breakfast beneath notice."

"Refuse not the gifts offered—You will doubtless use that

decanter of brandy in your coffee, for your stomachs sake and your many infirmities—Allow me ere you assume your seats, to introduce my respected brother Montmorency—long a fellow labourer in foreign climes—Brother O' Connor, a saved sinner—now a child of grace—If ever man had the root of the matter in him he has—('**** it'—growled poor O' Connor—sotto voce—'Its never shewn a sprout yet') Brother Quashia Quamina—I might even say—dearest brother (Here the Moor, without being aware, took two fire balls one after the other.) He is indeed a brand snatched from the burning"

O Connor had here nearly spoiled the play by suddenly vociferating "I'll be blessed—only look at him—if he is not burnt already!" —but a withering scowl from Mr Percy silenced the Slavers Captain—

"Excuse Brother O' Connor, my dear fellow laborours—He has put on the robe of godliness, but the old Adam now and then gives him a grip—Yet he is zealous my dear friends—he is zealous—My friends the native of the benighted land of Africa has been a chosen vessel for the evil one and after unheard of sins, brutalities, torturings —headings—hangings, roastings fleaings alive—burning man woman and child—crushing a thousand slaves into a one hundred ton slaver—in fact after having done all that Satan could do if let suddenly loose from Hell, He has become a burning and a shining light"

Here the three Wesleyans exchanged looks of exstatic delight—The idea of such heavenly converted sinners—of the thrilling experiences, the startling disclosures they would be able to give in the Chapel formed a prospect almost too rich; but poor Quamina so little understood his friends description of his character that nothing save Percys squinting glance prevented him from doffing his coat for a set-to on the spot.

"My beloved brother Mr Simpson" continued Percy "Is a Banker (Here the trio involuntarily rose to do homage) "but He holds his purse, and my brother only considers himself as a steward" (poor Jeremiah buttoned, at this part of the address, both breaches pockets) "My dear brother Gordon comes last—He has not been the least of sinners

—Hell has had hard hard hold upon him but he has escaped with the skin of his teeth—I never knew so great a reprobate or have seen so great a change! Indeed my Christian friends all in this room whom I have introduced to you have been the very vilest of sinners—Every crime of which human nature can be guilty, they have committed—every evil thought which could enter mans heart has blackened theirs; They have been eaten up with the filthiest sores of the souls leprosy—(Here O' Connor could hold no longer, but roared out 'I've a skin as fair as yours!') Excuse our brothers sailor like bluntness; it is only a little of the old leaven—there is not one of our dear brethren who ought not to be hung in chains long since—but thanks be to Him—they are now like lambs wool washed at the springs of Jordan!"

As 'The viler the sinner, the greater the saint' the three visitors looked up from plates filled a second time with the cold round—each giving a groan of intense satisfaction partly the result of a full heart and partly that of a full stomach. Mr Percy continued

"Brethren Providence hath given me a small endowment of carnal comforts—praised be His name—and I propose amid the sins and follies of this vanity fair, to devote my mite to the carrying out of the great work—So I shall request that you will allow me an open and lighted Chapel at 6 o'clock this evening, wherein a short missionary experience may be given you by my dear repentant brethren, and myself who am lower than the most ignorant sucklings in grace. I beg to place in the hands of my reverend brother in the bonds a small matter of this earthly dross to aid in printing bills and lighting the tabernacle of prayer."

So saying Mr Percy meekly deposited ten sovereigns in the hand of the Rev S. Slugg who trembled with the excess of his gratitude and looked at his benefactors boots as if he thought his tongue would be benefited by becoming their shoe black.

"You will oblige me—brother—a—a—whats your name?"

Slugg—Slugg—my dearest Sir!"

"Well—by drawing up a small bill for this evenings meeting"

Mr Slugg was not long ere his pen was flying fast and furious over a half sheet of paper, and in due time his labours produced—with a little assistance from Mr Momtmorency—the following veracious handbill.

"SANCTIFICATION CHAPEL.

Ardmore.

At 6 o'clock in the Evening of this day there will be held a special extraordinary meeting of the Wesleyan Missionary Society wherein light will be given from lamps fed with the oil of the ten virgins! The horrors of Sin—the iniquities of Heathenism—the cruelties of the slave trade—will be fully exemplified in the experience of several soul saved Sinners sanctified unto Salvation!

Those beloved brethren, once

lost and now restored—viz.

QUASHIA. QUAMINA.

Formerly a slave in Africa, then a slave driver—next a slave owner, and after wards a pirate captain—

ARTHUR. O' CONNOR.

who declares that he has been nearer to the arm pits in black and white blood than any sinner that ever Gods vengeance neglected to kick to Hell—

GEORGE. GORDON.

who solemnly declares that if he fully gave his experience the roof would fly from the best built Lords House in England—

JEREMIAH SIMPSON ESQr'.

The great Banker who taketh for his motto "Freely thou hast received— freely give'.

HECTOR. M. M. MONTMORENCY.

A humble gleaner in the harvest of souls

AND

ALEXANDER. PERCY. ESQR. M.P. PERCY HALL.

ALNWICK HALL. ELRINGTON HOUSE. HANTS. AND

NORTHANGERLAND HOUSE.

LONDON.

Who will lend to the aid of the Society his invalauble religious attainments—his untiring energies, his unequalled eloquence and his unparalleled benevolence.

Silver will most thankfully be received in the galleries, and friends who desire front pews will be expected to deposit 2s—6 into the hands of the Treasurer,

Simon Slugg.

N. B. The Classes will be called to prayer after the collection, when it is expected that A. PERCY. ESQR. MP. will address them."

"That will do" said Mr Percy as Hector with a ludicrous grin handed him the flattering expose of his companions former life and conversation —"Now my dear friends in the sacred cause, let this production be distributed extensively throughout the town and; 'ere evening put on the whole armour of righteousness, so that I—even I —David may with a sling and a stone slay the Philistine— even the man of sin—the old man Adam. Good Morning my dear brethren."

Thus, with a stately gesture, Mr Percy bowed his three confounded but triumphing visitors from the room—and then taking one other cup of Coffee dashed with brandy, he beckoned Hector to follow him and both departed either into another apartment, or on some confidential walk.

Those who remained behind, after a torrent of sighs and execrations, resigned themselves to stern fate, and swore that—black as they had been described, they would see the fun out though their usage was scurvy enough to turn a tortoise into a tiger.

"What shall we do—for I can only say 'unaccustomed as I am to public speaking' and I know the Bible as well as you know the Koran" remarked Mr Quamina sorrowfully looking at his Old Companion in arms

"The practical part of the affair is that I fear I shall begin by sending the whole chapel bodily to Hell—and then would'nt Percy storm a trifle!" answered O' Connor—but friendly advice was at hand for at this moment the waiter entered with a note addressed to the lachrymose gentlemen, which being opened proved to be in Hectors handwriting—

"The Vestry—Santification Chapel

Well, my beloved brethren—I always thought you were rogues but, till now I did not know that you were fools—But out of pity to your babyhood I'll just give you one fresh wrinkle in your strait—One fact is clear—that you must appear and speak unto improvement to night—But how are you to fructify when I question whether you ever opened the blessed pages since you first robbed your papa's orchard. Now mark me old fellows. Dress yourselves in black, or as our holy friend would say 'put on the whole armour of righteousness', sling round your thrapples a white neckercheif—and, when you are called on, LIE left and right as if according to the holy word you were lying "with a cart rope'. In blackening yourselves from your cradle to your conversion beat the powers of the imp who polishes the boots of Satan. If you can find words to picture earth as worse than Hell do so—but pray do not get too drunk ere you enter the sacred portal—I dont care about a dozen tumblers, but not one more except to Jeremiah who in consideration of his natural phlegm may be allowed the bakers or the devils dozen.

Remember boys our holy saint is in no joking mood to day—He is just now kneeling at a chair beside me screeching like a half throttled turkey **** for the lord. He roars so about crucifixion in Jesus that I wish from my soul he were nailed hand and foot like a dead magpie, to a barn door.

From your sinful travailer in the throes of labour, and about to bring forth a cubic yard of the blessed one—thus much.

N.B. If you wish to pull our holy friends delicate "petite nez retroussé" you may dash in a few stiffish hints respecting the sinful lusts of the flesh, and the pride of life—but alas you do not know the scriptural phraseology so I suppose I must do that myself!

The Rev H.M.M. Montmorency

Some time a feeble labourer in the vineyards of Damnblastaree—Swiglushaboo, and the torrid African wilds of Splitmytimberara" but now a labourer among the people called methodists.

To HIS servants

gathered over eggs

Ham Brandy and coffee

in the Breakfast room
Thurstons Arms."
"Grace and peace be with them"

"Well" said O' Connor with a sigh as if of gratitude for a mountain removed from his breast—"I see through it—The practical part of the evening will be just what I can weild, and if my lies don't kick down yon chapel Joshua's trumpets never floored the walls of Jericho!"

"I see no fun in the matter" returned Mr Quamina sulkily "He's a fool and he want[s] to make fools of us—I dont like to have my tail cut off to please the docked fox—But as you say Arthur I can LIE as far as from here to Guinea as as fast as the rapids of the Congo and as loud as a Gold Coast thunder storm. For not getting drunk to night I'll not promise, because I am so vexed at him."

Gordon only growled "I wish he would only think of women for he is never bearable when he deals with men" and Simpson muttered "I wish I may have the collection to count."

Some of my readers may know little of places of public worship except from such examples as they may find in the lofty roofed, nobly windowed piles which our national religion has dedicated to the service of God. But the decorous worship—the plain yet stately liturgy—the cathedral chaunts and those Anthems that speak to us from the graves of Purcell, Tallis, Gibbons, Bull, Kent or Green, find no parallel in the new raw cubes of brick or stone, pierced with two tiers of semicircular arched windows and possessed of interiors as fine as gaudily painted pews and galleries can make, which are denominated CHAPELS. These gems of classic architecture may possess Organs of much cost and enshrined in mahogany cases but, alas! their music is that of a waltz in 'delirium tremens' fancying that it is dancing souls to heaven; Their pulpits are adorned with unexceptionable velvet but the bibles lying upon them are thumped in time to a tattoo of extemporaneous raving: 'I speak not in anger but in sorrow' reader for though I could point out many an illustrious exception I have seen enough of what were once called 'conventicals' to feel aware that the slight sketch I have just drawn or the more finished picture which I mean to paint give no exaggerated idea of the follies into which man can plunge when he wishes to appear more holy than he is.

On the evening of the first day of Ardmore fair, Sanctification Chapel presented to the crowd assembled about its doors a blaze of gas light from every square paned window—Inside abundance of light threw a yellow glory over the rapidly filling pews and galleries, while a double lustre blessed the green baize-bordered platform erected for the distinguished orators in the forthcoming missionary meeting. Men with slouched shoulders and downcast eyes assiduously trimmed the lamps or scraped discordant preludes on violins and violoncello's[sic]—and perspiring but regenerated souls buried their faces in their hands under the influence of groaning prayer. The ladies too crowded fast into the scene of action with a very holy fervour though a sadly carnal attention to dress: Their upturned eyes and sadd[e]ned sighs' told of heaven but their satin bonnets and white handkerchiefs smelt a little 'of the earth, earthy'.

For a while the bare boards of the platform caused a feeling of impatience in the rapidly filling edifice but ere long those boards were pressed by the boots of five as beautiful specimens of sinners saved as ever trod upon Memel timber. The Rev H.M.M. Montmorency—The Rev J Simpson—the Rev G Gordon—the Rev A, O' Connor—the Rev Q Quamina—all attired in solemn sable took their seats amid the deepest groans among the male and with the liveliest sympathies from the female portion of the audience—and though the chosen presented countenances as rascally as ever faced the mob round Tyburn tree their erect gentlemanly figures and well whiskered manliness told well especially with the fairer and holier portion of the audience.

Mr Slugg followed these christian warriors and whispered a few words while he familiarily kept hold of the Rev Hectors Coat button but Montmorency audibly responded—

"My beloved fellow soldier wishes to fight the good fight himself —so he will both give out the hymn and probably lead on the Organ. On his knees this morning he vowed that the work should not be done slackly."

Ere he had ceased speaking the lion of the evening was seen making his way among a reverently parting crowd in the aisle; and, looking neither to the right hand or the left he ascended to his place, faced his audience and shewed to many a tenderly swimming eye a very tall shapely figure in solemn black with an aristocratic forehead shining in the gas light and a face whose angelic aspect was only marred by the accursed chestnut cuds and orange whiskers.

Waiting till an obligate movement of sighs and groans had ceased the Rev Alexander Percy began in a distinct but calm and silvery voice—

"My brethren and Sisters in Christ—I feel so much oppressed with the weight of a duty which a higher power has laid upon me that I request from you a song of prayer and praise ere we open forth the business of this evening—My brother Slugg I shall give out an hymn and accompany it on the Organ myself so it will be quite unnecessary for my Christian friend to make any use of the instruments I see in the music seat."

Slugg and the musicians could not forbear a look of very carnal mortification at the hauteur with which the holy man declined their assistance, but Montmorency covered his face with his handkerchief to hide the uncontrollable risibility which shook his ribs, as his experienced eyes saw the resolute determination on the part of his beloved friend to carry out the present farce with all the earnestness of his wayward and intractable character. Mr Percy, who if his wrapt and inspired eyes told [the] truth, had really seized the spirit of the hour, advanced to the front of the platform—waved his hand to still the troubled sea of groans and continued—

"Let us miserable worms send up our cry as if from Tophet in the following words and adapted to the tune of "Widdops 100th."

Before Our mighty Makers throne
Let us submissive kneel in prayer,
And strive for scarlet sins to atone
For we must pray that He may hear.
Deep—Mighty Lord—be our despair—
Distinct our consciousness of sin—

Lest from thine eyes our outside fan—
Should strive to hide our crimes within.
We know that we are formed for crime,
That through our lifetime crimes we form,
Believing, madly, all the time
That mercy shields us from the storm;
Or, as long since, in Shinars plain,
Rebellious men their Tower of pride
Raised up, in hopes, by labour vain
That thus thy power might be defied,
So we, by impious moral code
Or ever changing creeds of faith,
Think we may climb the narrow road,
Elude thy arm, and cheat our death.
But, Oh when we have gained Heaven's gate,
The eternal crown intent to win,
Long must we knock and, lingering, wait
Ere watching angels let us in!
"Hast thou repented of thy sin?"
What Soul—my God can answer then?
"Go back—Thy path again begin,
And weep and watch and wait again!"
But if returning be denied
By Deaths grim gateway, closed behind,
Where flies our heaven, our hope, our pride?
They fly like chaff before the wind!
Lord, let us know our treacherous mind
Even though that knowledge bring despair;
For, wandering thus, accursed and blind,
We dare not hope that Thou wilt hear!"

As I have already alluded to Mr Percy's musical powers I need hardly add now that when after giving out the hymn he took his seat at the Organ he soon sent the solemn harmony rolling through the chapel and ascending as if to heaven. Whatever the discomfited gut scrapers felt they were obliged to stare at [the] powers of the 'rich converted squire' and even the Rev S Slugg gave a groan of astonishment when the last deep chord had died away.

Mr Percy again advanced to the front of the platform and continued in what the soul saved declared were heavenly tones,

"My brethren God hath opened out a path through this worlds wilderness, and as to those who ask, much will be given, so to you who seek much will be found. We are nothing ourselves and by ourselves we can do nothing but guided by that Star which shone over Bethlehem more than eighteen hundred years ago and which now, if our dimmed eyes could see it, shines over Ardmore we may pursue a soldiers path and ere morning win a new victory over the hitherto unvanquished Man of Sin. I appear before you now as the advocate—the counsel in fact for a wide world brought before Gods bar for crime, and, and unless I successfully plead their cause condemned to a far worse punishment than any which human ingenuity can inflict—I plead for that wide land whose burning Sun blazes on bodies whose blackened hue is as snow compared with the midnight darkness of their Souls—I plead my brethren for Africa—I am counsel also in Gods court of justice for another land still wider—still older—still fuller of all associations which can rouse our hearts to the trumpet sound of human triumphs the funeral wail of human sorrows born—A land wherein our mortal nature found its cradle—wherein a young world met a watery grave —From which a world now called old had its dawning—out of one of whose lonely villages rose the star that has never sunk and whose bright beam from Bethlehem I will trust shines upon our meeting here. I plead for the earth that gave our first father existence and our Saviour a sepulchre—I plead my Christian friends for Asia. Another land also, with which from shorter acquaintance we have less sympathy demands your own and my attention—A land whose mighty rivers roll unknown and incalculable wealth to Ocean but which in itself is—save the United States—a wild and howling waste—nearly Four thousand miles of water draining a surface more than that of all Europe send hourly wasted wealth to the Atlantic and sorrowful sighs to heaven—The Amazons river preaches a sermon in every gush of its stream—The bones that whiten peruvian mountains cry aloud for vengeance—My Brethren I plead for America.

Another clime which God has favoured—which he has blessed with small gratitude received in return—a clime that has seized the reins and will direct the progress of earthly improvement—That clime too I must plead for—I plead for wealth changed to pride—power changed to tyranny—Religion changed to hypocrisy—Truth changed to falsehood—population changed to corruption—knowledge obtained only to work the deeds of darkness—I plead for EUROPE. And now my brethren must I not plead for the Island which gave me birth? For the land wherein lies all I have most loved on earth—among whose hills and vales my sorrowing body walks; beneath whose soil my weary head must rest— Must I not plead for our England—for our father land?"

Here Percy with eyes glistening and voice faltering under me influence of real though capricious emotions advanced to the very front of the platform and in still more earnest tones continued—

"The flesh that to my carnal mind was once worth all the world to me is now but an atom of thyself O world! The joy of my life is the sport of a worm! The anchor of my mortal back is torn away And now from rocks and quicksands who can save me—O Father! Only Thou! "For in thy hands is power and might, and Thou rulest and reignest over all!" Yet England—my country demands a warmer expression of feeling than any I can give to far off lands, for that place which all we love most fills our arms or their graves we must think of oftenest—love the most, and with the most agony deplore—Forgive me, my Christian brethren—I wander from an important text—"Go ye forth and preach the gospel in my name." Yes let us go from the north and the south, to the uttermost Isles of the sea—Let His word mingle with the sound of waters that heralds Lena and Obi and Eniseei to their cold Siberian Sea—Let it return in "iron knell" from the mighty peaks that separate dreary Thibet from fertile India—Let it wake the slumber of America with a voice louder than the thunders of her Andes—Let it tell unhappy Africa that the wide waves of her Nile or her ***** can never fertilize her thirsty sands till their waters unite with the sacred stream of Jordan.

Upon the banks of that river our souls will all in Gods due time have to stand, with the Ægypt of this worlds happiness and the wilderness of this worlds sorrow left like Israels forty years of wandering behind us—With the deep and treacherous flood beneath us—With the unclouded blaze of Heaven before us!—

That,

"When we tread the verge of Jordan"

we may have no need to fear that its waters will hurry us toward the sea of Sodom, but that guardian angels with white wings waving over a sunlit shore will give us a helping hand to place our feet on for ever flowering meadows. Is the earnest soul felt prayer of one who has wandered long in an inward Arabia and who now humbly prays that Yourselves and himself may reach a happy Canaan.

My Brethren excuse further speech from me at present; Brother Montmorency will introduce the speakers and open the real business of the meeting much more ably than myself—I feel I am nothing and have said nothing.

May HE have pity on us all!"

The Rev A Percy with a general bow to the enraptured audience took his seat amid a flourish of five hundred white handkerchiefs. The Male portion of the assembly groaned deeply but the female portion felt deeply, and if a keen observer had noticed the odd half smile on Percys mobile lips as he looked round after taking his seat he would have known at once that the Orator had known to whose feelings he ought to address himself and to whom he meant to feel indifference.

When the tempest of groans, sobs, sighs, and screamings had somewhat subsided the Revd Hector. M.M. Montmorency rose and with his blacksmith arms folded across a breast as broad as Ben Caunt's and his wild Irish eyes glinting like black diamonds in a coal mine he burst forth in tones like the bass of La blache

"Well my fellow warriors Brother Percy has just given you a screed of sound doctrine but it's too fine my lads—Its too fine—We poor sinners want a good scouring out ere we are clean—A point lace towel won't do for us—rough horse hair and brooms instead of brushes are the real remedy for our accumulated monstrosities upon case hardened consciences. Now I have here two real horse combs made of cast iron and ready as cheese maggots to jump where Jesus calls them (You perhaps have never yet seen maggots spang off a knife into your mouth but I have) Well these two have been the biggest scamps that ever donned a shirt, and they now are the holiest saints that ever gave orders for a pair of wings—They are sure to have them my brethren—when they leave this misguided world—They are ready for them in heaven's warehouse—full feathered, and every quill tipped with gold. Think of the difference between their hopes and yours if you do not alter—pinions like Archangel Michael's for them—Hoofs like Archangel Lucifer's for you—Alter then my lads—make no gingerbread matter of it—Never did worse devils live than the two brothers who will now address you, and if they have passed the verge of Jordan why may not you?

Look to the lord my lads—fight the great enemy, though he had as many lives as a cat, and let me introduce to you—Captain Arthur O' Connor—once too worthless to have a coal wasted in roasting him and now galloping toward heaven as fast as Baalam's ass can carry him"

At the conclusion of this eloquent speech the Barrister took a pinch of snuff—hid his face to conceal indecent laughter which was working within him like beer in a barrel, and motioned O' Connor to rise.

With a very reluctant movement and a very irreligious curse the wild eyed, red haired sea officer obeyed the signal—the more quickly from seeing Percy squint—He stood irresolute with perspiring cheeks for a minute and then as if his mind were made up he struck both fists on the front rail of the platform and dashed at once "in medias res"—

Its no use my friends—I am a man unlearned in Godliness, and I have known the old one better than ever I knew my own father or Mother—I have never been worthy of conversion but I have been tumbled into Salvation—Neck and heels you percieve my friends—Glory be to God! Well I suppose I must tell you a bit of my experience—I came from a rich Irish family living at the rate of not more than £2000 per annum above their income but being an elder son I saddled the estate privately with some few debts to be paid off—interest meanwhile to accumulate—when the old Governor should die. Glory be to God, he lived to see me cut my creditors and take to the high seas—Oh had I but taken to salvation!" (Here tremendous groans for some time interrupted the orator) "Well thats a hit any how! Now then my lads—I mean my Christian brethren—I landed on the Gold Coast with a soul blacker than the body of any devil incarnate that ever bartered mans flesh for a fifteen shilling musket! I did by ("stop stop' said Montmorency sotto voce.) Well, never mind—I'll let you into the secrets of life before that clock strikes eight—I spent all my first capital in buying slaves, and as King Boy of old Calabar—You knew King Boy Quashia?"

"Aye that I did Arthur! The old De—I mean brute would have diddled me out of as fine a lot of real Bambarra niggers as ever were thrust under hatches merely because no more than two out of thirty of my best 15s Birmingham muskets would go off at the first fire. I told him it was the climate, to which they were not yet seasoned, but the Old boy was not to be done."

A dreadful squint from the Revd. A. Percy placed a padlock on the Moor's tongue, and the Revd. A. O' Connor continued—

"Well—my lads—that is—my dearest brethren—this King Boy said that if I would "dash him" he would trust me for a ton or so of elephants teeth I consented to visit his majesty—Now, mind you, 'dashing' means oiling the palm—and the best dash is an anker of brandy or a keg of new rum—Well I dashed his majesty with two big calabashes of as fine red raw rum as ever scalded a mans entrails—It was beautiful to see his white eyes rolling, and his black paws patting his pursy paunch (there's alliteration for you Hector!) as he gradually stowed his hold with the leeward-Island stuff till he had got as good a cargo on board as a man need wish to leave port with. "Golly massa" he sputtered "Me no hab done dis while—Me spew, and den see what me do!" Well the old fellow being sick at the stomach essayed to leave the hut—beg pardon—I mean palace—and as his vessel lurched, and tacked as if against a head wind I thought it my duty to take him in tow as a steam tug would a dismasted tub of a collier. Hang me but when I touched him the graceless unrepentant sinner gave me a right handed lunge which would have sent me sharply over the streams of Jordan had not a New Testament which I had in my waistcoat pocket saved me— Yes my blessed Brethren—My Testament saved me! May it save you too!"

The tumultous groans of joy which broke from the hitherto bewildered congregation made Percy aware that one other word from his eloquent colleague would only spoil the good hit he had made, so hastily stepping forward he said loudly—

"My Christian friends, the hour waxes late, me day is far spent—perhaps to some among us the night may be at hand—My brother O' Connor is exhausted with previous labour—I introduce to relieve him—my dear brother Quashia Quamina."

The copper-coloured gentleman advanced to the front of the platform with precisely the same aspect as would have been assumed by him if taking a last look on this weary world from the elevation of Newgate scaffold.

"Blasted ******* and brothers—confound you Hector, don't kick my shins so—I mean Ladies and Gentlemen—now that's too bad Hector—well, Christian friends, then—Unaccustomed as I am to public speaking, and I'll be most cruelly expliflicated if I ever stood on any platform save the deck, before, I will try to enlighten the gentiles and give them some insight into the goings on in our business; I mean—d'ye mind me—what was our business once—Well—where was I—Percy, you unhanged villain I won't be trailed by you any longer!"

Furiously turning to the Revd A Percy, the irascible Moor muttered an oath and resumed his seat, but the cheif actor in the evening's farce, without noticing his colleague's eccentricity, stepped forward and addressed the audience with a forehead like an Indian ocean in a summer calm.

"My dear friends and fellow Christians the zeal of my fellow labourers has eaten them up, and I much fear that the affecting disclosures which their experience would compel them to make would be painful to their tender feelings as well as to your own: I shall therefore adjourn this meeting till a future evening, and may He protect you all from the burning hill that was ready to fall upon Christian—from the stones that struck the vital breath out of holy Stephen—from the gridiron that fried St. Lawrence—from the crucifixion, head downwards, that gave apoplexy to St Peter—from the roasting of Polycarp—from the impetuous pride of Tertullian—from the vanity of Athanasius—from the laughing atheism of Lucian—from the humbugs of Plato, the treachery of Judas, the plagiarisms of Virgil, the repetitions of Homer,"

"Halt," cried Montmorency "What on this earth are you driving at?" But Percy nothing heeding 'drifted on his path' and certainly 'with silence deep as death' him—

"Yes, from the fate of Alcibiades' dog's tail from the fate of Prynne's ears, from the fate of Charles the first's head and of Oliver Cromwell's nose from the falsehood of Psalmanazer and Jacob, from the impudence of Colonel Blood, and Joab, from the vanity of Absalom and the young Pretender, the go and come virginity of my Ancestress Queen Elizabeth, the death of my pretty Queen Mary, the hard heartedness of Brutus, the clemency of Titus that crucified fifty Jews round the walls of their city, the charity of Inquisitors general—Malay pirates, Slave drivers—I do not allude to my two regenerated fellow labourers present— From the tender mercies of Henry VIIIth and George IVth, of Henry VIIth and old Elwes, of Prince Rupert and the Marquis of Waterford, of Chateaubriand and Robert Montgomery—of Prince Marshal Blucher and Bernard Barton, from all these terrors, Good Lord deliver us!"

As the Revd Alexander Percy concluded with a look of which canvass could give no transcript—Mr Montmorency took his hand gave out a hymn, led the dismayed congregation through the last round of their dance of enthusiasm and all left the chapel impressed with the idea that the Revd. A. Percy was a very odd but very apostolic saint.

Percy departed without another word for his mind did not happen to be under the roof which sheltered his body. O' Connor and Quamina sat stroking their hair from their foreheads, and Mr H.M.M. Montmorency enjoyed the happiness which a warhorse may have while galloping over the dying and the dead.

In a while O' Connor wiping the perspiration from his face sighed forth—

"Well, Quashia, what the deuce are we to do now? That accursed Daguerreotype of Lucifer has got his Barometer up to 120° in the shade, and you know how little we liked that pitch when we had scarce a hand left to handle a rope off that pompous peice of Portuguese humbug. Fort Elmina, and that regular mantrap 'Cabo Corso' castle."

"I'de rather hang out the red flag within range of Cape Coast Castle guns than sit where I am doing Arthur."

"Now my lads" broke in the Irish Banister with a glorious chuckle "I move that "plase the pigs' you—

—"Dont go home till morning;

Till daylight doth appear."

for then Alexander the great, seeing your red eyes and pallid cheeks, will deem you repentant, and in his tender mercy forgive you."

"E'gad it's a good suggestion!" exclaimed the culprits in a breath — though Quashia remarked with an oath that if Percy shewed any tender mercies he must have borrowed them at heavy interest from Simpson, for he was sure he had not a farthing' s worth of his own.

"Never you mind where he gets his mercies more than he does where he gets his lasses so long as they are there." said Hector.

"And Echo answers—where?" replied Quashia.

The lamps in the emptied Chapel were flickering amid the smell of their approaching dissolution—the stars seen through the windows were fast outvying them, and shewed that Heaven is seen more distinctly as Earthly light declines.

Montmorency led his legion into the still crowded streets and what they did during the 'sma' hours' of that night—"Is it not written in the books of the Chronicles of the Kings of Israel?!

The first visitor to the Coffee room of the Hotel, next morning, was the Hero of the previous night, who entered with a look, half quizzical—half serious—and rang the bell which was answered by Fanny.

"Fanny—what do they think of me in these parts?"

Fanny blushed, giggled and replied

"Why Sir, they say you are a very nice looking gentleman."

"Ah, but that is not to the point—It's the Soul, Fanny, that I'm thinking of! What do they say about my soul?"

"Well—really—Sir—Why we do not know what to think—We think you are a great gentleman and a clever one—and you pay well —and people say Sir—people say—"

"What—Fanny?"

"Well—do excuse me Sir—They say you have behaved ill to women often."

"Ah! My girl—remember that the tongue though it be a little member can work great mischeif! I'm as innocent as a new born babe —Get me a cup of coffee—four poached eggs, and a 'demi tasse' of Cogniac for breakfast."

"What is that last order Sir?"

"It means as much Brandy as you please my girl—I thought you understood the Chaldaic dialect of the Hebrew—But you perhaps understand that language." said Mr Percy—impressing an unmistakable kiss on the pink cheek of the young woman, who left the room to execute his orders in a rather flurried and hesitating manner.

As she closed the door his eyes wandered to the window through which beyond the houses could be seen the purple summits of the moorland hills. A long line of fir plantations marked the spot wherein his feelings anchored, and as soon as he had dispatched a hasty breakfast, to that spot he wended his way.

The mild but rather misty air of the uplands for a while diverted his mind from the follies of the previous night. The cattle quietly lying in their mornings rest among the dew spangled grass and half opened daisies, the mountain sheep with shackled limbs still contentedly making their breakfast on the produce of an ungrateful soil, all spoke of calm and contentment—sincere, though perhaps forced, and shewn by objects humble enough in the scale of Creation.

The being of a far mightier mind, and compared with whom, every living thing round his path was little better than would have been the vitality of a polypus, walked forward, sometimes smiling at the little bits of English scenery which no one save Bewick has ever copied on wood or steel, but far oftener casting the mental eye backward upon an object of love long laid in her grave, or forward, upon one whose grave he might be the means of making.

There are hours when our thoughts take in, and fully comprehend years as well as minutes; when the long chain which connects bygone, with present and with forthcoming years blazes like one vivid streak of lightening, and gives mans feelings almost a prophetic power to look into his future doom.

Such a power Mr Percy seemed to have obtained when he leaned on the gate of the avenue leading to Darkwall and thought of the Mary he had lost, and the Maria he was to meet.

After his eye had wandered a while over whitey green pastures and storm beaten moors he entered the Hall, and in its Breakfast room met the beautiful though melancholy looking mistress of the mansion

The old fashioned room with its Elizabethan windows and its roof pointed from the centres to the octagonal diverging supports did not attract his attention, but the Lady who welcomed him did—She entered with a took of studied solemnity, but with a shining in the eyes that said solemnity might sometimes tell lies.

Mrs Maria Thurston had known enough of sorrow, and God had intended her to both know and feel enough of love. She had before her a man capable of exciting every feeling that a woman can know—She had, as the possessor of her own person, a man, if I can write him down as such, who could not gain more than momentarily—her feelings, and who never could fill them at all. She had lost thoughts of him except in her ideas of dread of him, and so many years had elapsed since he had bestowed on her even one moment of, I fear, selfish fondness, that the remembrance of her bridal days caused the astonishment which one feels when thinking that ones childhood took for truth the gibberish of a nursery tale.

Now, and for long ago she knew that on rising she must dress to face a day of duties performed unthanked and, so far as her thoughts were concerned, objectless care.

What was it then that caused an expression to cross her face which even the servant who closed the door could notice, as Mr Percy greeted her with a tight rein upon his tongue but a hot spur within his mind? Whatever she felt an unusual visitant—colour—invaded her cheeks as she replied to his greeting of "Well Madam—

There is an unseen power which draws us onwards"

So in accordance with Schiller's philosophy I am hither thus early from the coarseness of Ardmore cattle fair."

"I suppose Sir you have yet been so kind as to do your utmost to correct that coarseness for I have understood that Mr Thurstons guest performed—positively for one night only in the Methodist Chapel at ——"

"Oh do not speak of it! You do not know me—When I am most inwardly serious I am most outwardly absurd—Last nights folly was a borrowed cloak to shelter me from the passing storm and to be returned when the blast should have hurried it by. It has not been the first occasion on which I have dressed myself in motley, but I can doff the fools cap as easily as don it—Why do you look so sad?"

"I did not know that my looks were changed from their usual character—But I am sure Sir that after the eccentricities of last night you will need refreshment this morning—more especially as I suppose you mean to spend the day on the moors."

"Maria—Madam, I mean—No, **** it, it shall out—Maria—I do not mean to spend the day on the moors—I am no sentimental milk-sop, and I like a day spent at the tail of a pointer or a foxhound as well as any fellow that ever donned a green or scarlet Jacket, but I have other likings, and I would rather bring down sorrow from a well loved face than wing the finest Bustard (if there is one left) on the plains of Wiltshire. I know you are unhappy Maria—Yes you may put on the mockery of a smile and look as though you would say you were not—but your lot in life has been among thorny paths and against inclement skies. God made you by nature to be all that a woman could be, so far as her sunshine can enlighten a blighted world—You have been made, by some other power not very nearly akin to God, no better than a weed tossed on the water I can see it and if I wish to strive for a few hours to cheat you out of the bitter consciousness of your fate impute my wish not to a sin on my part, but to tenderness for her who instead of being a weed tossed on the water ought to be a jewel worn in a crown."

"Sir—Sir—Remember who I am—and for my sake forbear to—"

"I remember I know well enough what thou art—I know the earthquake ground on which I tread—But, Maria, through distress and danger to come— through hours of self reproach that I am too stubborn to own to others—through scenes that make me sick of my life—thou shalt—thou must be now my guiding star. Do not let those tears run down thy cheek unless I am to kiss them off—Do not play with and look at thy eye glass as if it and not Alexander Percy were talking to thee—Remember, my Maria, that we stand on a point of time— sorrow has been behind us both—The balm of mutual love may be before us—for I know that thou lovest me, and thy words need not put themselves to the trouble of a denial—and if we must part—Maria—remember a rough villain amid all his mental storms will have one sweet harbour in which that mind may anchor—An ill used lady will find that when she has to retire to a lonely room from the conclusion of thankless toils—she may, ere she lays her head on a (I would hope) peaceful pillow—feel that one man—up to all both of the good and evil of life—and who never prays for himself, is praying most unselfishly for her."

Some of my readers may think that the foregoing report of the breakfast room conversation sounds overstrained, or rhapsodical, but as I only

"tell the tale as 'twas told to me"

and can with the mental eye see plainly the noble looking, passionately feeling, well experienced and highly talented scoundrel standing over, and warmly regarding the mild, sweet tempered, but sorrow stricken lady, who (save in this new attraction for her feelings) saw nothing through future life save continual travel over stony roads —I can tell them that the talk was not the kernel, but the shell, and that, after a look of almost vindictive fierceness, one close embrace gave to Mr Percy's arms one whom, at that hour he could not have lived without—and who in the whirl of her own feelings knew not whether she were dead or alive.

With cheek, now white, now red she sat beside Mr Percy, whose light complexioned countenance altered no more than did his orange whiskers but he pressed her dark curls to his bosom and said

"Maria—You must take a walk in the park or plantation—You look sickly, and my arm will be a good support during your walk—Don't be frightened to take the arm that of all the 2,000,000,000 arms in this world would be the first to protect thy dear little self. Now I shall bring thy bonnet and veil and mantle out of the entrance hall and I insist upon thy putting them on—so wipe thy eyes, my love, and believe that this hand which rather roughly grasps thy neck would be a powerful defender if any other hand dared grasp it"

Mrs Thurston—powerless under the impulse of contending feelings, mechanically walked into the hall and returned ready for a morning walk, but with her sweet confiding eyes looking, now at the powerful past, then at the awful future.

Seeing that she hesitated in entering Percy threw open the window which admitted of immediate access to the lawn, and taking her arm first, and next her waist compelled her by his impetuosity of will to resign herself to his direction during the mornings walk.

The Breakfast Room was left empty now, and the forenoon sunshine beamed as usual upon the customary display of old Furniture and uncouth china. The grim portrait of Mr Thurston frowned over the mantle piece. The fair, but wan looking lady of the mansion smiled sorrowfully from her gilded frame, beside it, but the image of the man who was fated to change the destinies of that house was not there. His lofty forehead, orange whiskers, and sarcastic mouth were not to be found in the gloomy brow, black complexion, and purely malignant aspect of William Thurston.

While the room was empty of living occupants, times gone by, perhaps, looked down from the walls as forty centuries looked down from Cheop's pyramid upon the victory of the "Sultan Kebir" over the chivalrous Mamelukes; But the room was not long empty for, ere long, in burst the brawny, Irish form of Hector. M.M Montmorency—while Mr H.M.M. Montmorency was tenderly enquiring from a servant after the welfare of his dear friend Alexander—Mrs Thurston and her guest entered through the still opened window which invited ones footsteps from the sward without.

Mrs Thurston's raven tressess were rather disordered—and Mr Percy's azure eyes twinkled very suspiciously so Mr Montmorency, with bowels yearning as much as ever Jacob's or David's did for Benjamin or Jonathan— advanced toward his lofty friend and fervently exclaimed—

"Oh, I love thee! I do like that squint—It is so very amiable!"

Then turning as if he had not been aware that Mrs Thurston had entered the apartment, Mr Montmorency apologized for his rough outburst of friendship, and earnestly longed to know if Mrs Thurston were well, and able to traverse the moors that day!

Mrs Thurston answered the Irish Barrister as shortly as possible and, as much as possible, without a glance at his dark searching countenance. Mr Percy recklessly keeping beside his fair hostess on the sopha threw a look at Hector, such as would have given one lightning blaze from the Silla de Carracca's to the port of Cumana. A stranger, ignorant of human nature might have been puzzled to explain the meaning of the triumphant brightness of the gentleman's glance or tell the reason for the perpetual check which he seemed forced to keep upon his usually voluble tongue, while addressing Mrs Thurston. Indeed once, when she was taking from the table a very large folio of local Antiquities to shew it to Montmorency he so far forgot himself as to say imperiously and warmly

"Halt, Darling—I'll carry it"

and as she coloured violently and could not speak, while he muttered "**** those slips of the tongue!" Montmorency's snuff box came into requistion and it might have been observed that his scrutiny of the architectural engravings and coats of Arms was as inquisitive as could have been the gaze of Dr Dryasdust or Jonathan Oldbuck but the Irish eyes were noticing, from their corners the changing cheek of the lady, and the cockles of his heart "rejoiced to find that she could not tear herself from that sofa and allowed Percy's hand to fall upon her own without noticing the 'accident'.

Looking at the plan of a Roman Camp alleged to have been discovered on the adjacent moors Montmorency remarked in a mild voice

"I always admire a commander who can kick aside your gradual approaches and take a fortification by storm. Zigzag work will do for the practice of the law, but it does not look natural or prove sucessful in war or in Love. to be sure a Spider would hardly agree with me, for it is very wary in catching its fly—but then when it has got it—who so brisk as the spider?"

As Mr Percy only answered by the pantomime of a sneering laugh, and the growling observation that a spider could kill a wasp, Mr Montmorency continued—

"Well, now, to business. You must know, however painful it may be to disclose the secret—and, believe me from the testimony of this bleeding bosom that it is a pain from which only burning tears could relieve me—a pain that no issue to the event, however happy, could wholly remove—for it lies here!"

"If you mean the inside coat pocket I judge it to be an unmanageable brief

"Oh no! professional business must lie asleep now!"

"Thank Heaven! Now Mar—Madam we may hope for happiness when Law sleeps."

"Oh Percy

'Alas, I feel I am no actor here!'

Our beloved fellow labourers, our fellow soldiers under His banner, our pilgrim companions, our virgin sisters, those who have fought under the cross by our side and who may with us eventually win and wear a martyrs crown, are—but how can I declare it in your presence Madam—They are in quod!"

Mrs Thurston evidently did not understand the Banisters peroration and her mild eyes asked from Percy's face an explanation of the awful word; but that face, instead of consternation, expressed ecstatic pleasure as its lips whispered

"At last they are at home!"

"Oh but my friend" pleaded the Banister "think of the wives—stop they are not married—well then, of their children, poor little souls, sent adrift on the stormy ocean of this world—"

"Egad! They have been adrift since they were hatched Mat!"

"Well, but their mothers—"

"What? The childrens mothers, or the Saint's Hector?"

"You are not yet out of the shell—I mean the bonds of Satan—Percy. Do you know that Quashia and O' Connor are in the lock up, and will be brought this morning before Thurston and—worst of all—before Sir John Sinclair!"

On hearing that last name Mrs Thurston's pale cheek turned yet paler and she asked

"Then has my uncle arrived from Scotland?"

"He has—because he foresaw the evil to come like a double sighted Highlander as he is!"

Percy frowned on the lady as he noticed her change of countenance and then rose, turning to Montmorency with the remark that he supposed the poor devils wanted bail and he was sure that neither Jerry or Gordon would give it without a consideration so he supposed he must go down to Ardmore—'but' he concluded, as he left the room with his friend I shall be back with your hus—with Thurston."

Mrs Thurston stood alone in the room, and as she saw the tall athletic gentleman in the dark green Newmarket Coat ride off by the side of his danger boding companion she involuntarily clasped her hands and exclaimed

"Oh God! My life is changed!"

Forethoughts of events to come gathered round her like tide

waves round a stone, and like such waves overwhelmed her. Consciousness of what she has done that morning flashed like lightning through her soul, and though one thud of her mind prayed for God's mercy and another third enquired, "had she sinned at all!' the last third compelled he to fall on her knees, bury her face in the sopha cushion, and utter, amid sobs and at intervals, her scarcely coherent prayer.

"Oh God forgive me if thou cans't! I do not know how much I have angered thee—I do not know whether or not I sin in daring to pray to thee—I only know that I cannot help myself, that I am going whither my every feeling leads me, and that, come what may, into thy hands I must fall. The world will now judge ill of me—My sisterhood will shun me—Snares will surround me—my life will be endangered, a long dark future may be preparing for me and Hell itself may rise to meet meat my comings; But how can I shake off what my heart clings to? How can I vow to thee that I will forget him who seems all I have hoped for and never have obtained? How can I return to silent submission under heartless tyranny and keep any promise to hate the name of love?

I loved this world—I longed to see it happy—I did all I could to please whom I could—I gave myself to one who promised what he did not perform—I still kept to my promises and smiled away sorrow when I could, or hid it when misery overmastered the smile—Through all I felt blameless and could each night place my trust in Thee. What, then, can I do now? I cannot hate him—I cannot forget him—He has made me love him, and yet I must cast his image aside or live, a traitor to my vow, and a sinner in thy sight.

"My God, I cannot cast him aside! I should lie if I promised it—I long to be his own,but I have, through my life longed to be Thine own. I cannot be both, and now I must try to long to be in my grave.

Where, my God, is thy compassion, and why is it denied to me? Am I doomed to an endless agony; and, if so, wherefore am I doomed? I am as thou hast formed me—I feel as thou hast caused me—I act as thou permittest—I suffer what thou willest—I am thine with whom to do what thou pleasest— but—I am another's also!

Forgive me if I pray for him this night when I shall not dare to pray for myself. Forgive me if my eyes turn from the daily repeated scene of sorrow to the seldom coming hour of joy. I ask Thee to forgive me but I dare not hope it, so I must entirely trust myself to my darkening fate and to Thine own almighty power!"

Mrs Thurstons white forehead and raven curls were turned toward heaven as she rose with streaming eyes—she dried them with a white handkercheif which she thought her own, but flushed as she noticed the letters "A.P." in the corner, and then hurriedly left the room to try to fulfill her duties.

PART IV

THE LETTERS OF BRANWELL BRONTË

A NOTE ON THE TEXT

The letters that follow are produced as comprehensively as possible, and I have edited only where necessary for clarity. A detailed context to each of them is beyond the scope of this book, but I have provided commentary where appropriate.

1

TO THE SECRETARY OF THE ROYAL ACADEMY - JULY 1835

SIR,

Having an earnest desire to enter as Probationary Student in the Royal Academy but not being possessed of information as to the means of obtaining my desire I presume to request from you as Secretary to the Institution an answer to the questions –

Where am I to present my drawing?

At what time –?

And especially

Can I do it in August or September?

Contrary to popular belief, there is no evidence that Branwell was sent to the Royal Academy, nor evidence that he even applied. In fact, there are a few tiny lines of script on the reverse of this letter, suggesting it was a discarded draft.

2

TO WILLIAM ROBINSON - 16TH NOVEMBER 1835

DEAR SIR,

After repeated delays, for which I am ashamed to apologise I have at length nearly completed my picture, and shall be ready to appear with it before your bar of judgement on Monday next the 23rd of this month. But should this day prove inconvenient to yourself, my Father desires me to request that you would name by Letter any day and time you may think proper; since that which would be the most convenient to you would certainly prove the same to me.

And my Father likewise, being so sensible of the value of your instructions and so pleased with your manner of conveying them, has resolved upon my receiving (if it should prove agreeable to you) a course of Lessons during the ensuing Winter, in addition to those you have already given me – but upon this subject it may be most proper to speak when I see you Sir; which time is looked forward to with no little fear and doubting by – if he dare aspire to the title

Your Obedient Pupil

P B Brontë

William Robinson was an artist with a studio in nearby Leeds. Robinson had studied at the Royal Academy, and been a pupil of Sir Thomas Lawrence, painter-in-ordinary to the King. Branwell's letter was rewarded with a number of lessons which ultimately led Branwell to a short-lived career in portrait painting.

3

TO THE EDITOR OF BLACKWOOD'S MAGAZINE - DECEMBER 1835

AND WOULD TO HEAVEN YOU WOULD BELIEVE IN ME, FOR THEN YOU would attend to and act upon it!

I have addressed you twice before, and now I do it again. But it is not from affected hypocrisy that I begin my letter with the name of James Hogg; for the writings of that man in your numbers, his speeches in your *Noctes*, when I was a child, laid a hold on my mind which succeeding years have consecrated into a most sacred feeling. I cannot express, though you can understand, the heavenliness of associations connected with such articles as Professor Wilson's, read and re-read while a little child, with all their poetry of language and divine flights into that visionary region of imagination which one very young would believe reality, and which one entering into manhood would look back upon as a glorious dream. I speak so, sir, because as a child 'Blackwood' formed my chief delight, and I feel certain that no child before enjoyed reading as I did, because none ever had such works as *The Noctes, Christmas Dreams, Christopher in his Sporting Jacket* to read. And even now, 'Millions o' reasonable creatures at this hour-na', no at this hour', etc. 'Long, long ago, the day on which she died. That hour so far more dreadful than any hour than can darken us on earth, when she, her coffin and that velvet pall descended, and descended slowly, slowly into the horrid clay, and we were borne deathlike, and wishing to die, out of the churchyard that from that moment we thought we could never enter more.' Passages like these, sir (and when that last was written my sister died)-passages like these, read then and remembered now, afford feelings which, I repeat, I cannot describe. But one of those who roused these feelings is dead, and neither from himself nor yourself shall I hear him speak again. I quiver for his death, because to me he was a portion of feelings which I suppose nothing can rouse hereafter: because to you he was a contributor of sterling originality, and in the *Noctes* a subject for your unequalled writing. He and others like him gave your Magazine the peculiar character which made it famous; as these men die it will decay unless their places are supplied by others like them. Now, sir, to you I appear writing with conceited assurance: but *I am not*; for I know myself so far as to believe in my own originality, and on that ground to desire admittance into your ranks. And do not wonder that I demand so determinedly: for the remembrances I spoke of have fixed you and your Magazine in such a manner upon my mind that the idea of striving to aid another periodical is *horribly repulsive*. My resolution is to devote my ability to you, and for God's sake, till you see whether or not I can serve you, do not coldly refuse my aid. All, Sir, that I desire of you is that you. would in answer to this letter request a Specimen or Specimen's of my writing and I even wish that you would name the subject on which you would wish me to write – In letters previous to this I have perhaps spoken too openly respecting the extent of my powers, But I did so because I determined to say what I believed; I know that I am not one of the wretched writers of the day, I know that I possess strength to assist you beyond some of your own contributors; but I wish to make you the Judge in this case and give you the benefit of its decision.

Now Sir, do not act like a common place person, but like a man willing to examine for himself. Do not turn from the naked truth of my letters but prove me – and if I do not stand the proof I will not farther press myself on you – If I do stand it – Why – You have lost an able writer in James Hogg and God grant you may gain one in

Patrick Branwell Brontë

All the Brontë children were avid readers of Blackwood's Magazine, and Branwell made a number of attempts to secure admission into its hallowed pages. All of them were unsuccessful. He received no reply to any of his letters.

4

TO THE EDITOR OF BLACKWOOD'S MAGAZINE - 8TH APRIL 1836

THE AFFAIR WHICH ACCOMPANIES MY LETTER IS CERTAINLY SENT FOR insertion in 'Blackwood' as a Specimen which, whether bad or good, I earnestly desire you to look over; it may be disagreeable, but you will thus KNOW whether, in putting it into the fire, you would gain or lose. It would now be impudent in me to speak of my powers, since in five minutes you can tell whether or not they are fudge or nonsense. But this I know, that if they are such, I have no intention of stooping under them. New powers I will get if I can, and provided I keep them, you, sir, shall see them.

But don't think, sir, that I write nothing but Miseries. My day is far too much in the morning for such continual shadow. Nor think either (and this I entreat) that I wish to deluge you with poetry. I send it because it is soon read and comes from the heart. If it goes to yours, print it, and write to me on the subject of contribution. Then I will send prose. But if what I now send is worthless, what I have said has only been conceit and folly, yet CONDEMN NOT UNHEARD.

5

TO THE EDITOR OF BLACKWOOD'S MAGAZINE - 4TH JANUARY 1837

In a former letter, I hinted, that I was in possession of something the design of which, whatever might be its execution, would be superior to that of any series of articles which has yet appeared in Blackwood's Magazine – But, being prose, of course, and of great length, as well as peculiar in character, a description of it by letter would be impracticable. – So surely a journey of 300 miles shall not deter me from a knowledge of myself and a hope of entrance into the open world.

Now, Sir, all I ask of you is – To permit this interview, and, in answer to this letter, to say that you will see me, were it only for one half hour – the fault be mine should you have reason to repent your permission.

Now, is the trouble of writing a single line, to outweigh the certainty of doing good to a fellow Creature and the possibility of doing good to Yourself? – Will you Still so wearisomely refuse me a word, when You can neither know what you refuse or whom you are refusing? Do you think your Magazine so perfect that no addition to its power would be either possible or desirable? – Is it pride which actuates you – or custom – or prejudice? – Be a Man – Sir! and think no more of these things! Write to me – Tell me that you will receive a visit – and rejoicingly will I take upon myself the labour, which, if it succeed, will be an advantage both to you and me, and, if it fail, will still be an advantage, because I shall then be assured of the impossibility of succeeding.

6

TO WILLIAM WORDSWORTH - 10TH JANUARY 1837

SIR,

I most earnestly entreat you to read and pass your judgement upon what I have sent you, because from the day of my birth to this the nineteenth year of my life I have lived among wild and secluded hills where I could neither know what I was or what I could do. – I read for the same reason that I eat or drink – because it was a real craving of Nature. I wrote on the same principle as I spoke – out of the impulse and feelings of the mind; – nor could I help it, for what came, came out and there was the end of it, for as to self conceit, that could not receive food from flattery, since to this hour Not half a dozen people in the world know that I have ever penned a line. – But a change has taken place now, Sir, and I am arrived at an age wherein I must do something for myself – the powers I possess must be exercised to a definite end, and as I don't know them myself I must ask of others what they are worth, – yet there is no one here to tell me, and still, if they are worthless, time will henceforth be too precious to be wasted on them.

Do pardon me, Sir, that I have ventured to come before one whose works I have most loved in our Literature and who most has been with me a divinity of the mind – laying before him one of my writings, and asking of him a judgement of its contents, – I must come before someone from whose sentence there is no appeal, and such an one he is who has developed the theory of Poetry as well as its Practice, and both in such a way as to claim a place in the memory of a thousand years to come.

My aim, Sir is to push out into the open world and for this I trust not poetry alone that might launch the vessel but could not bear her on --- Sensible and scientific Prose bold and vigorous efforts in my walk in Life would give a farther title to the notice of the world and then again Poetry ought to brighten and crown that name with glory – but nothing of all this can be even begun without means and as I don't possess these I must in every shape strive to gain them; Surely in this day when there is not a writing poet worth a sixpence the field must be open if a better man can step forward.

What I send you is the Prefatory Scene of a much longer subject, in which I have striven to develop strong passions and weak principles struggling with a high imagination and acute feelings, till, as youth hardens towards age, evil deeds and short enjoyments end in mental misery and bodily ruin. Now, to send you the whole of this would be a mock upon your patience; what you see does not even pretend to be more than the description of an imaginative child. But read it, sir; and, as you would hold a light to one in utter darkness as you value your own kind-heartedness return me an answer, if but one word, telling me whether I should write on, or write no more. Forgive undue warmth, because my feelings in this matter cannot be cool; and believe me, sir, with deep respect, your really humble servant,

P. B. BRONTE

Branwell enjoyed no better success with Wordsworth than he did with Blackwood's; he received no reply to his letter. The 'Prefatory Scene' he sent was the poem 'Still and bright, in twilight shining', a fascinating subversion of Wordsworthian themes that, unfortunately, went unpublished. You can, however, read it in 'The Poems of Branwell Brontë'

7

TO JOSEPH BENTLEY LEYLAND - 1837

My Dear Sir,

I only enclose the accompanying fragment, which is so soiled that I would have transcribed it if I had the heart to exert myself, in order to get from you as to whether, when finished, it would be worth sending to some respectable periodical like Blackwood's Magazine.

I trust you got safely home from rough Howarth and am,

Dear Sir,

Yours most sincerely,

P.B.Brontë

The letter itself is not dated, but the fragment Branwell refers to was a poem titled 'Percy Hall'. Undeterred by the silence he met from Blackwood's, he sought the aid of Joseph Bentley Leyland, a sculptor he had met while painting portraits in Bradford. Perhaps he hoped to make use of Leyland's connections - Leyland's father had previously printed and published The Halifax Guardian, *which was known for publishing poetry.*

8

TO JOHN BROWN, SEXTON OF HAWORTH - 13TH MARCH 1840

OLD KNAVE OF TRUMPS,

Don't think I have forgotten you, though I have delayed so long in writing to you. It was my purpose to send you a yarn as soon as I could find materials to spin one with, and it is only just now that I have had time to turn myself round and know where I am. If you saw me now, you would not know me, and you would laugh to hear the character people give me. Oh, the falsehood and hypocrisy of this world! I am fixed in a little retired town by the sea-shore, among wild woody hills that rise round me – huge, rocky, and capped with clouds. My employer is a retired county magistrate, a large landowner, and of a right hearty and generous disposition. His wife is a quiet, silent, and amiable woman, and his sons are two fine, spirited lads. My landlord is a respectable surgeon, and six days out of seven is as drunk as a lord! His wife is a bustling, chattering, kind-hearted soul; and his daughter! – oh! death and damnation! Well, what am I? That is, what do they think I am? A most calm, sedate, sober, abstemious, patient, mild-hearted, virtuous, gentlemanly philosopher, – the picture of good works, and the treasure-house of righteous thoughts – Cards are shuffled under the tablecloth, glasses are thrust into the cupboard, if I enter the room. I take neither spirits, wine, nor malt liquors, I dress in black and smile like a saint or martyr. Everybody says, 'What a good young Gentleman is Mr Postlethwaites tutor!' This is fact, as I am a living soul and right comfortably do I laugh at them. I mean to continue in their good opinion. I took a half-year's farewell of old friend whisky at Kendal on the night after I left. There was a party of gentlemen at the Royal Hotel, and I joined them. We ordered in supper and whisky-toddy as (hot as hell ! ' They thought I was a physician, and put me in the chair. I gave sundry toasts, that were washed down at the same time, till the room spun round and the candles danced in our eyes. One of the guests was a respectable old gentleman with powdered head, rosy cheeks, fat paunch, and ringed fingers. He gave ' The Ladies/ . . . after which he brayed off with a speech; and in two minutes, in the middle of a grand sentence, he stopped, wiped his head, looked wildly round, stammered, coughed, stopped again, and called for his slippers. The waiter helped him to bed. Next a tall Irish squire and a native of the land of Israel began to quarrel about their countries; and, in the warmth of argument, discharged their glasses, each at his neighbour's throat instead of his own. I recommended bleeding, purging, and blistering ; but they administered each other a real ' Jem Warder/ so I flung my tumbler on the floor, too, and swore I 'd join 'Old Ireland!' A regular rumpus ensued, but we were tamed at last. I found myself in bed next morning, with a bottle of porter, a glass, and a corkscrew beside me. Since then I have not tasted anything stronger than milk-and-water, nor, I hope, shall, till I return at Midsummer ; when we will see about it. I am getting as fat as Prince William at Springhead, and as godly as his friend, Parson Winterbotham. My hand shakes no longer. I ride to the banker's at Ulverston with Mr. Postlethwaite, and sit drinking tea and talking scandal with old ladies. As to the young ones ! I have one sitting by me just now fair-faced, blue-eyed, dark-haired, sweet eighteen she little thinks the devil is so near her!

I was delighted to see thy note, old squire, but I do not understand one sentence you will perhaps know what I mean. . . . How are all about you? I long to hear and see them again. How is the ' Devil's Thumb' whom men call __ __, and the 'Devil in Mourning' whom they call __ __. How are __ and __, and the Doctor; and him who will be used as the tongs of hell - he whose eyes Satan looks out of, as from windows - I mean __ __, esquire? How are little, __ __, __ 'Long-shanks', __ __ and the rest of them ? Are they married, buried, devilled, and damned ? When I come I'll give them a good squeeze of the hand ; till then I am too godly for them to think of. That bow-legged devil used to ask me impertinent questions which I answered him in kind. Beelzebub will make of him a walking-stick ! Keep to thy teetotalism, old squire, till I return ; it will mend thy old body. . . . Does ' Little Nosey think I have forgotten him? No, by Jupiter! nor his clock either. I'll send him a remembrance some of these days! But I must talk to some one prettier than thee; so good-night, old boy, and believe me thine,

THE PHILOSOPHER.

Write directly. Of course you won't show this letter; and, for Heaven's sake, blot out all the lines scored with red ink.

Many Brontë scholars have pointed to this letter whenever they want evidence as to Branwell's terrible ways. They will often quote parts of it but, now that you have read the whole thing, I imagine you will agree with me that, in fact, this letter is more proof of Branwell's wild imagination than anything else.

This letter was written during Branwell's employ as a tutor for Robert Postlethwaite, a prominent landowner in the Lake District. Branwell had been hired to provide Postlethwaite's sons with a classical education.

Branwell spent just six months in Postlethwaite's employ, and it is unclear why he was dismissed. However we cannot read too much into this letter.

His description of the 'regular rumpus' reads so much like a bawdy Angrian drinking scene, which in turn are imitations of Byron's own bawdi-

ness, that it is impossible to credit it as truth. Branwell calls himself 'the devil', but there is no evidence that he was any 'threat' to women.

Rather than revealing any dark secrets, it is far more likely that this letter is Branwell's attempt to impress John Brown, a man who was thirteen years his senior. Were Branwell truly a wild Byron of Haworth, would he ask that certain lines be blotted for fear of being seen by his family?

9

TO HARTLEY COLERIDGE - 20TH APRIL 1840

SIR,

It is with much reluctance that I venture to request, for the perusal of the following lines, a portion of the time of one upon whom I can have no claim, and should not dare to intrude; but I do not, personally, know a man on whom to rely for an answer to the question I shall put, and I could not resist my longing to ask a man from whose judgement there would be little hope of appeal.

Since my childhood I have been wont to devote the hours I could spare from other and very different employments to efforts at literary composition, always keeping the results to myself, nor have they in more than two or three instances been seen by any other. But I am about to enter active life, and prudence tells me not to waste the time which must make my independence; yet, sir, I love writing too well to fling aside the practice of it without an effort to ascertain whether I could turn it to account, not in wholly maintaining myself, but in aiding my maintenance, for I do not sigh after fame and am not ignorant of the folly or the fate of those who, without ability, would depend for their lives upon their pens; but I seek to know, and venture, though with shame, to ask from one whose word I must respect: whether, by periodical or other writing, I could please myself with writing, and make it subservient to living.

I would not, with this view, have troubled you with a composition in verse, but any piece I have in prose would too greatly trespass upon your patience, which, I fear, if you look over the verse, will be more than sufficiently tried.

I feel the egotism of my language, but I have none, sir, in my heart, for I feel beyond all encouragement from myself, and I hope for none from you.

Should you give any opinion upon what I send, it will, however condemnatory, be most gratefully received by, Sir, your most humble servant,

P. B. BRONTË.

P.S. The first piece is only the sequel of one striving to depict the fall from unguided passion into neglect, despair, and death. It ought to show an hour too near those of pleasure for repentance, and too near death for hope. The translations are two out of many made from Horace, and given to assist an answer to the question would it be possible to obtain remuneration for translations for such as those from that or any other classic author?

Where Branwell failed to garner a response from Blackwood's or from Wordsworth, he succeeded with Hartley Coleridge. The son of Samuel Taylor Coleridge, Hartley was a poet too (although a far less successful one). Branwell included with his letter some poetry as well as some of his attempts to translate Horace's Odes. *The latter impressed Hartley, and Branwell was invited to spend the day with the other poet.*

10

TO HARTLEY COLERIDGE - 27TH JUNE 1840

Sir,

You will, perhaps, have forgotten me, but it will be long before I forget my first conversation with a man of real intellect, in my first visit to the classic lakes of Westmoreland.

During the delightful day which I had the honour of spending with you at Ambleside, I received permission to transmit to you, as soon as finished, the first book of a translation of Horace, in order that, after a glance over it, you might tell me whether it was worth further notice or better fit for the fire.

I have – I fear most negligently, and amid other very different employments – striven to translate 2 books, the first of which I have presumed to send you, and will you, sir, stretch your past kindness by telling me whether I should amend and pursue the work or let it rest in peace?

Great corrections I feel it wants, but till I feel that the work might benefit me, I have no heart to make them; yet if your judgement prove in any way favourable, I will re-write the whole, without sparing labour to reach perfection ... Excuse my unintelligibility, haste, and appearance of presumption, and – Believe me to be, Sir, your most humble and grateful servant,

P B Brontë

If anything in this note should displease you, lay it, sir, to the account of inexperience and not impudence.

This letter was written after Branwell had been dismissed from the Postlethwaite's employ and had returned to Haworth. Unfortunately, there is no evidence that Branwell received a response, although a draft of Hartley's response survives.

11

HARTLEY COLERIDGE TO BRANWELL BRONTË - 30TH NOVEMBER 1840

Dear Brontë

I fear you have thought me unkind or forgetful in neglecting so long to notice your letter and the enclosed translations. Believe me, I would not be the one, and could not be the other – but I am a sad Procrastinator ... You are by no means the first or the only person who has applied to me for judgement upon their writings. I smile to think that so small an asteroid as myself should have satellites. But you have heard the distich –

Fleas that bite little dogs have lesser fleas that bite em –
The lesser fleas – have fleas still less – so on – ad infinitum.

Howbeit, you are – with one exception – the only young Poet in whom I could find merit enough to comment without flattery – on stuff enough to be worth finding fault with. I think I told you how much I was struck with the power and energy of the lines you sent before I had the pleasure of seeing you. Your translation of Horace is a work of much greater promise, and though I do not counsel a publication of the whole – I think many odes might appear with very little alteration. Your versification is often masterly – and you have shown skill in great variety of measures – There is a racy English in your language which is rarely to be found even in the original – that is to say – untranslated, and certainly untranslateable effusions of many of our juveniles, which considering how thorough[ly] Latin Horace is in his turns of phrase, and collocation of words – is a proof of sound scholarship – and command of both languages – languages we will - will you please examine a few odes–odes critically–critically analytically.

The first is not one of Horace's best, and I must say that it is your worst. Whatever merit is has in the original, is in the precise word, and juncture– juncture which our language cannot ever compensate. That Mecaenas, atavis edite regibus–regibus Horace set about of malice prepense to cast the infirmities of our old mother lingo in her teeth–teeth could not have done it more provokingly. For what is the English of Atavus? Great-great-great grandfather! There is no language which I know the least of–of is so miserably off for terms of lineage as ours. Pater–Pater-Proavus–Proavus-Atavus Tritavus, is a line of Plautus which it would be impossible to render into any modern language. I do not know whether Horace meant to compliment Mecaenas with that precise degree of descent from the Etruscan Monarchy but your–your of kingly line–line far too weak and vague. The feeling is much the same as if you were to address a welsh squire as a descendant of Caractacus or Howel Dha.

Oh Davy Dean, sprung from the blood
That was true Welsh before the flood
And royally from sire to son
Descended ere the world begun–

I once essayed to imitate the Ode in an irregular metre–metre after this fashion–

Mecaenus–Mecaenus of kings renownd in story–
At once my sure defence, and pleasant glory–
Here we that have a might past

For trophies of Olympic dust
When the glowing wheels have nicely turned
The goal and the palm is nobly earnd
Nobly earned and justly given
It lifts the Lords of Earth to Heaven–

Although this is a letter written to Branwell, not by him, I felt it worth including. If anything, it is a relief that someone *was planning to reply to one of his many attempts to reach out to someone in the world of words. And reply with praise! It would be too much to suggest that Branwell's life would have been drastically different if Hartley had finished and sent this letter. But I imagine it could have given Branwell some of the positive encouragement that he sorely needed.*

12

TO JOSEPH BENTLEY LEYLAND - 15TH MAY 1842

DEAR SIR,

I have received great pleasure from the examination of the three Drawings which you put in to the hands of Mr J. Brown, and it appears to me that the Design at £40.

No. 2.

has received the greatest approbation from the Committee appointed to carry into effect the erection of a monument to the late Mr Andrews

If you could come over to Haworth on the Afternoon of Friday May 20th; during the evening of which day the Committee will sit, they will be able to speak more distinctly to you than I have power to do - and I am sure my Father would be pleased to see you if you can make it convenient to visit us before the meeting.

Mr Brown will be thankful for any instructions you may be pleased to give him, and as he expects an order for two more monuments - of course through your hands - he will be thankful for some information respecting the best method of colouring letters Sunk in marble tablets.

Excuse the extreme illegibility of this scrawl as I am scarcely

~~hoping~~ recovering from severe indisposition, and, with a hope to see you on Friday,

Believe me,

Dear Sir,

yours most respectfully,

P.B. Brontë

P.S.

I should feel obliged by knowing per return of post whether it will be in your power to come over on the day mentioned above, or not.

Resurgam

13

TO FRANCIS GRUNDY - 22ND MAY 1842

Dear Sir,

I cannot avoid the temptation to cheer my spirits by scribbling a few lines to you, while I sit alone – all the household being at church – the sole occupant of an ancient parsonage, among lonely hills which probably will never hear the whistle of an Engine till yourself and I are in the grave.

After experiencing, since my return home, extreme pain and illness, with mental depression worse than either, I have at length regained health strength and soundness of mind far superior, I trust, to anything shewn by that miserable wreck which you used to know under my name. I can now speak cheerfully and enjoy the company of another without the stimulus of six glasses of whiskey: I can write, think, and act with some approach to resolution; and I only want a motive for exertion to be happier than I have been for years before: But I feel my recovery from almost Insanity, to be retarded by having nothing to listen listen to except the wind moaning among old chimneys and older Ash Trees – nothing to look at except heathy hills walked over when life had all to hope for and nothing to regret with me – no one to speak to except crabbed old Greeks and Romans who have been dust these two thousand years: And yet this quiet life –

from its contrast, makes the year passed at Luddenden foot appear like a Night mare; for I would rather give a hand than undergo again the grovelling carelessness – the malignant yet cold debauchery – the determination to find out how far the mind could carry the body without both being chucked into Hell, which marked my conduct while there – lost as I was to all that I really liked; and seeking relief from the indulgence of feelings which form the black spot in my character.

The rapidity of my recovery from such a state of ruin proves – I trust that I have still something left in me which may do me service, but I ought not to remain too long in solitude, for the world soon forgets a man who has bidden it 'goodbye'; and, though quiet is an excellent cure for a diseased mind, no medicine should be continued after the patient's recovery.

Convinced of the necessity, and anxious for the opportunity of active life, I am about – though ashamed of the business – to dun you for an answer to the following questions.

1st – Can I obtain a chance of some situation, under English Engineers, on one of the lines commencing abroad, either in Russia – Sweden – Belgium – France – or the Sardinian Dominions – such as I could properly fill, if possessed of the qualifications mentioned below – viz.

The usual branches of a gentleman's education – including some acquaintance with French and such a notion of Drawing and the execution of plans &c as might perhaps with proper instruction be turned to some useful account in office or out of door employment.–

Recommendations from any necessary number of individuals, and these of the most respectable order.–

Securities to any amount requisite.–

Excuse the trouble I am giving to one on whose kindness I have no claim, and for whose services I am offering no return except gratitude and thankfulness, which are already due to you. A word or two to show that you have not altogether forgotten me will greatly please,

Dear Sir,

Your most obdt Sevt,

P.B.Brontë.

Give my most sincere and respectful regards to Mr Stephenson, to whom I should have written, but that I am not inclined to trouble anyone with more of my correspondence than I can avoid.

Branwell had met Grundy while working at Luddenden Foot railway station. Branwell was dismissed after an accounting irregularity, but this letter shows that he was eager to secure another position on the railways.

14

TO FRANCIS GRUNDY - 9TH JUNE 1842

DEAR SIR, ANY FEELING OF DISAPPOINTMENT WHICH THE PERUSAL OF your letter might otherwise have caused, was allayed by its kindly and considerate tone; but I should have been a fool to entertain, under present circumstances, any very sanguine hopes respecting situations connected with Railways; since I could not but be aware of the great glut in that market.

I had only hoped that, from the few who are generally found willing to take them, and from so many Railways being contemplated, in France &c; situations abroad would be more attainable.

You ask me, Sir; why I don't turn my attention in another direction? and so I would but that most of my relations, and more immediate connections, are Clergymen, or, by a private life, somewhat removed from this busy world – And, as for the church, I have not one mental quality – except perhaps hypocrisy – which would make me cut a figure in its pulpits.

Mr James. Montgomery, and another literary gentleman, who have lately seen something of my 'head work', wish me to turn some attention to literature, sending me, along with their advice, plenty of puff and praise; and this may be all very well; but I have little conceit of myself, and great desire for activity. You say that you write with feelings similar to those with which you last left me; keep them no longer. I trust I am somewhat changed, or should not be worth a thought; and though nothing could ever give me your buoyant spirits and an outward man corresponding therewith, I may, in dress and appearance, emulate something like ordinary decency. And now, wherever coming years may lead Greenland's snows or sands of Africa I trust, etc.,

PATRICK B. BRONTË.

15

TO JOSEPH BENTLEY LEYLAND - 29TH JUNE 1842

Dear Sir,

I think it is my duty to send to you a copy of the inscription intended for Mr Andrew's monument.

If it is not such a one as would have best pleased myself, but I was compelled to frame it so as to please others; as to whose taste and judgement you will some time since have formed a tolerably correct opinion.

I have not often felt more heartily ashamed than when you left the committee at Haworth; but I did not like to speak on the subject then, and I trusted that you would make that allowance which you have perhaps often ere now had to do, for gothic ignorance and ill breeding; and one or two of the persons present, afterwards felt that they had left by no means an enviable impression on your mind.

Though it is but a poor compliment - I long much to see you again at Haworth, and forget for half a day the amiable society in which I am placed, where I never hear a word more musical than an asses bray; When you come over bring with you Mr Constable, but leave behind Father Matthews; as his conversation is too cold and freezing for the comfort among the moors of Yorkshire.

Trusting soon to see you; I remain, Dear Sir,
Yours respectfully and sincerely,
P.B. Brontë.

16

TO JOSEPH BENTLEY LEYLAND - 12TH JULY 1842

DEAR SIR,

Mr John Brown understands from Mr Newsholme of Haworth, who lately called upon you & that you will be prepared to bring the Tablet hither on ~~Sat~~ Friday; and he wishes to know whether it will be your pleasure to do so, and thus have the letters blackened and all completed under your own eye; or whether you intend that he shall bring it over to Halifax on Saturday and complete it there?

He would also be much obliged by being informed whether or not it will injure the work to clean the slab from the yolk laid on it, before it is blackened.

An answer early enough to give him power to act as you think proper will much oblige him.

Expecting with pleasure the hour when I shall see you, I remain, Dear Sir, Yours sincerely, P.B.Bronte

Northangerland has so long wrought on in secret and silence that he dare not take your kind encouragement in the light which vanity would prompt him to do.

P.S. Can you state whether in your best monuments it has been usual to insert the stops or not. P.B.B

17

TO JOSEPH BENTLEY LEYLAND - 10TH AUGUST 1842

DEAR SIR,

Mr John Brown begs to ask, through me, whether you would be kind enough to send him, by an early opportunity, a small quantity of materials for blacking and removing the colour from white marble; as he has some lettering now on hand.

Your work at Haworth has given to all who have seen it the most unqualified satisfaction even where they understood nothing of its real merit; and of that crew you must expect more than of any other.

When you see Mr Constable - to whom I shall write directly - be kind enough to tell him that - owing to my absence from home when it arrived, and to the carelessness of those who neglected to give it to me on my return - I have only now received his note. Its injunctions shall be gladly attended to; but he would better please me by refraining from any slurs on the fair fame of Charles Freeman, or Benjamin Caunt Esqrs[1]. Yours, most respectfully & sincerely, P. B. Brontë

1. Charles Freeman and Benjamin Caunt were both boxers in the 1840s. Branwell was a keen follower of boxing.

18

TO FRANCIS GRUNDY - 25TH OCTOBER 1842

MY DEAR SIR, There is no misunderstanding. I have had a long attendance at the death-bed of the Rev Mr Weightman, one of my dearest friends, and now I am attending at the death-bed of my aunt, who has been for twenty years as my mother. I expect her to die in a few hours.

As my sisters are far from home, I have had much on my mind, and these things must serve as an apology for what was never intended as neglect of your friendship to us.

I had meant not only to have written to you, but to the Rev. James Martineau, gratefully and sincerely acknowledging the receipt of his most kindly and truthful criticism at least in advice, though too generous far in praise ; but one sad ceremony must, I fear, be gone through first. Give my most sincere respects to Mr. Stephenson, and excuse this scrawl my eyes are too dim with sorrow to see well. Believe me, your not very happy but obliged friend and servant,

P. B. BRONTË.

19

TO FRANCIS GRUNDY - 29TH OCTOBER 1842

MY DEAR SIR, As I don't want to lose a real friend, I write in deprecation of the tone of your letter. Death only has made me neglectful of your kindness, and I have lately had so much experience with him, that your sister would not now blame me for indulging in gloomy visions either of this world or another. I am incoherent, I fear, but I have been waking two nights witnessing such agonising suffering as I would not wish my worst enemy to endure; and I have now lost the guide and director of all the happy days connected with my childhood. I have suffered such sorrow since I last saw you at Haworth, that I do not now care if I were fighting in India or _, since, when the mind is depressed, danger is the most effectual cure. But you don't like croaking, I know well, only I request you to understand from my two notes that I have not forgotten you, but myself.

Yours, etc.,

P. B. BRONTË

20

TO JOHN BROWN - MAY 1843

Although the letter no longer exists, extracts were made by Lord Haughton from the original in 1859. The letter itself was written from Thorp Green, where Branwell and Anne had been hired as tutors and where Branwell would meet Lydia Robinson. As these words are not taken directly from the original, they should be taken with a pinch of salt.

In May 1843 he writes from Mr Robinson's near York – (Thorpe) to say he is living in a palace, with a delightful pupil – I curl my hair & scent my handkerchief like a Squire – I am the favourite of all the household – my master is generous – but my mistress is DAMNABLY TOO FOND OF ME She is a pretty woman, about 37. with a darkish skin & bright glancing eyes. – He asks his friend seriously to advise him what to do – tells him to consult two other grave men, who will understand him. is it worth-while for him to go on to extremities, which she evidently desires – the husband is sick & emaciated – she is always making him presents, talking to his sister (the governess) about him – telling him she does not care a farthing for him – asking him if he loves her & so on

21

TO JOHN BROWN - NOVEMBER 1843

Lord Haughton made another extract from a letter which, again, no longer exists.

In November 1843 he writes regretting that he has not seen some Haworth friends – 'I know you think I drink, but the time is past when I could hold out against you all. I take no wine & brandy & water only once in the day – that is, before breakfast to enable me to face the AGONY of the day' 'My little lady grows thinner every day – she is full of spirit & courage, except in the thought of parting with me.' He abuses a Methodist Preacher, who is told if he says anything to damage him (B. B.) he shall be ruined & Miss Anne Marshall saw him do enough to hang him. He sends his friend a 'lock of her hair, which has lain at night on his breast – would to God it could do so legally!' he ends in great depression – without signature.

22

TO JOSEPH BENTLEY LEYLAND - 4TH AUGUST 1845

Dear Sir,

John Brown wishes to know whether, or not, you can make your intended visit to Haworth this week.

Of course he awaits, and will be ready for your own convenience, in naming your week or your day.

I need hardly add that I shall myself be most delighted to see you, as God knows I have a tolerably heavy load on my mind just now, and would look to an hour spent with one like yourself as a means of at least, temporarily, lightening it.

I returned yesterday from a week's journey to Liverpool and North Wales, but I found during my absence that wherever I went a certain woman robed in black, and calling herself "MISERY" walked by my side, and leant on my arm as affectionately as if she were my legal wife.

Like some other husbands, I could have spared her presence.

Yours most sincerely, Brontë

By this time, Branwell has been dismissed from Thorp Green. He claims that this is due to his having become involved with Lydia Robinson, the wife of his employer. Branwell claimed to be tortured by his inability to be with Lydia, but there is not much evidence to suggest there was, in fact, any such affair. It's possible that Branwell invented the affair to give himself a more Byronic air.

23

TO JOSEPH BENTLEY LEYLAND - 19TH AUG 1945

My dear Sir,

John Brown wishes to know whether the payment due for the monument will be most acceptable this week, as, if so he can get it from the parties before Saturday and give it into your hands.

They had not the required sum in the house or he would have received it today.

The Tablet has fully satisfied all who have seen it.

As to my own affairs I only wish I could see one gleam of light amid their gloom.

You I hope are well and cheerful. Yours sincerely P.B.Brontë

24

TO JOSEPH BENTLEY LEYLAND - 10TH SEPTEMBER 1845

My Dear Sir,

I was certainly sadly disappointed at not having seen you on the Friday you named for your visit, but the cause you allege for not arriving was justifiable with a vengeance - I should have been as cracked as my cast had I entered a room and seen the labours of weeks or months destroyed (apparently - not, I trust, really) in a moment.

That vexation is I hope over and I build upon your renewed promise of a visit; for nothing cheers me so much as the company of one whom I believe to be a MAN, and who has known care well enough to be able to appreciate the discomfort of another, who knows it too well.

Never mind the lines I put into your hands, but come hither with them, and if they shall have been lost out of your pocket on the way, I won't grumble, provided you are present to apologise for the accident.

I have, since I saw you at Halifax, devoted my hours of time snatched from downright illness, to the composition of a three volume Novel - one volume of which is completed - and along with the two forthcoming ones, has been really the result of half a dozen by past years of thoughts about, and experiences in, this crooked path of life.

I felt that I must rouse myself to attempt something while roasting daily and nightly over a slow fire - to while away my torment and I know that in the present state of the publishing and reading world a Novel is the most saleable article so that where ten pounds would be offered for a work the productions of which would require the utmost stretch of a man's intellect - two hundred pounds would be a refused offer for three volumes whose composition would require the smoking of a cigar and the humming of a tune.

My Novel is the result of years of thought and if it gives a vivid picture of human feelings for good and evil - veiled by the cloak of deceit which must enwrap man and woman - If it records as faithfully as the pages that unveil mans heart in Hamlet or Lear the conflicting feelings and clashing pursuits in our uncertain paths through life I shall be as much gratified (and as much astonished) as I should be if in betting that I could jump over as I should be if in betting that I could jump over the Mersey I jumped over the Irish sea. It would not be more pleasant to light on Dublin instead of Birkenhead than to leap from the present bathos of fictitious literature onto the firmly fixed rock honoured by the fact of a Smollet or Feilding.

That jump I expect to take when I can model a rival to your noble Theseus who haunted my dreams when I slept after seeing him - but meanwhile I can try my utmost to rouse from almost killing cares, and that alone will be its own reward.

Tell me when I may hope to see you and believe me, dear Sir, Yours, P.B.Brontë.

A sketch is included in the letter, captioned with 'Bendigo 'taking a sight.' Alas! Poor Caunt!'

25

TO RICHARD METCALFE - OCTOBER 1845

Dear Sir,

I respectfully beg leave to offer myself as candidate for the situation of Secretary to the Manchester and Hebden Bridge and Keighley and Carlisle Junction Railway.

I trust to be able to produce full testimonials as to my qualifications and Securities, if required, to any probable amount.

I am,
Dear Sir,
Your most respectful and obedt Servt,
P.B. Brontë

Richard Metcalfe was a solicitor based in nearby Keighley and was acting as the local agent for a planned railway that would connect Manchester, Hebden Bridge, and Keighley Junction. While many have painted Branwell as a refusing to seek further employment after Thorp Green, this letter proves that Branwell was still seeking gainful employment.

26

TO FRANCIS HENRY GRUNDY - OCTOBER 1845

DEAR SIR,

I fear you will burn my present letter on recognising the handwriting, but if you will read it through you will perhaps rather pity than spurn the distress of mind which could prompt my communication after a silence of nearly three (to me)eventful years.

While very ill, and confined to my room, I wrote to you, two months ago, directing my letter to either the principal Inn in Bingley or Keighley, because I did not know your proper address; and as I heard you were engaged on the Bradford extension line I concluded that in your surveys you would have occasion to take your quarters at times in either of the two houses. I never heard from you in reply and as my letter only asked for one day with you to ease a very wearied mind in the company of a gentleman who use to have what I wanted always, but most want now-cheerfulness-I am sure you never received my letter or your heart would have prompted an answer.

When I say that since I last shook hands with you in Halifax two summers ago my life till lately has been one of apparent happiness and indulgence you will ask why should I now complain? And I can only reply by shewing the undercurrent of distress that bore my bark toward a whirlpool despite the surface waves of life that seemed wafting me toward peace.

In a letter begun in the spring of 1848 and never finished owing to incessant attacks of illness I tried to tell you how I was situated. As Tutor to the only son of a wealthy gentleman whose wife was sister to Mr Thos Gisborne M.P. for Nottingham and Mrs Evans the wife of the member for one division of Derbyshire. and the cousin of Mr. Macaulay. This lady (though her husband detested me) shewed toward me a degree of kindness which when I was deeply grieved one day at her husbands conduct opened into an unexpected declaration of more than ordinary feeling. My admiration of her mental and personal attractions which, though she is 17 years older than myself, are both very great, my knowledge of her totally unselfish generosity, sweet temper and unwearied care for all others with ill requital in return My horror at the heartless and unmanly manner in which she was treated by an eunuch like fellow who though possessed of such a treasure never even occupied the same apartment with her. All combined to make me reciprocate an attachment I had little dared to look for. During nearly three years I had daily "Troubled pleasure soon chastised by fear" in the society of one whom I must, till death, call my wife.

Three months since, while at home, I received a furious letter from my Employer threatening to shoot me if I returned from the vacation- and letters from her ladies maid and her physician informed me of the outbreak and threatened proceedings only checked by her firm courage and resolution that come what might harm might to her none should come to me. The wretchedly broken health and want of energy in her bloodless mock husband made him put up with the simple joy of daily torturing her while I was left uninjured.

Had I strength to return and meet him the results would be serious to one or both, but providence has hitherto denied me this power for I have lain during nine long weeks utterly shattered in body and broken down with mental despair. The probability of his state of health ere long leaving her free to give me herself and her estate as was her hearts resolve never rose to drive off the prospect of her decline under her present grief and sufferings and I dreaded too the wreck of my mind and body which God knows have both during a short life been severely tried.

Eleven continued nights of sleepless horrors reduced me to almost blindness and while taken into Wales to rouse me the sweet scenery, the sea, the sound of music only caused fits of unspeakable distress and irrepressible tears. I implored for society and comfort but could neither be pleasant to one or pleased by the other, and wine or other stimulants only caused not exhilaration but deeper dejection.

You will say "What a fool!" but if you knew the many causes I have had for sorrow which I cannot hint at here you would pity as well as blame.

I am better now but though at the kind request of Mr Macaulay and Mr Baines I have striven to rouse my mind by writing something that I ought to make deserving of being read, I find I really cannot yet do so with effect for one line of poetry like one note of music produces in my frame a sickening thrill of despair.

I know you will - if you read it at all - despise this letter and its writer, but I can only answer the writer does the same, and he would not wish to live if he did not hope that active exertion and change of scene may yet restore him to the by past manhood which used to boast of unconquerable health, where for 3 year he has known no interval of one week from agonising sickness, and latterly not even one day.

I should indeed be gratified if I knew that you would soon be anywhere where an hours visit to you would not be forbidden.

The crumpled appearance of the sheet is owing to my having kept it unfinished for days in my pocket.

Apologising sincerely for what will seem whining egotism and hardly daring to hint about days when in your company I could sometimes laugh or smile the thoughts of which

"Remind me of departed times"

but, I would fain hope, not
Departed never to return."

I remain,
Dear Sir,
Yours most sincerely,
P.B.Brontë.

27

TO JOSEPH BENTLEY LEYLAND - 25TH NOV 1845

My Dear Sir,

I send through yourself the enclosed scrap for the Halifax Guardian - and I ought to tell you why I wish anything of so personal a nature to appear in print.

I have no other way, not pregnant with danger, of communicating with one whom I cannot help loving. Printed lines with my usual signature "Northangerland" would excite no suspicion - as my late unhappy employer shrunk from the base idea of my being able to write anything, and had a day's sickness after hearing that Macaulay sent me a complimentary letter so He won't know the name.

I sent through a private channel one letter of comfort in her great and agonising present afflictions, but I recalled it through dread of the consequences of a discovery. The lines only have one merit, that of really expressing my feelings while sailing under the Welsh mountains - when the band on board the steamer struck up "Ye banks and braes" - and God knows that, for many different reasons, those feelings were far enough from pleasure.

I suffer very much from the mental exhaustion which arises from brooding on matters useless at present to think of - and active employment of thought would be my greatest curse and blessing - for really after hours of thoughts which business would have hushed I have felt as if I could not live, and, if long continued, such a state will bring on permanent affection of the heart which is already bothered with most uneasy palpitations.

I should like extremely to have an hours sitting with you, and if I had the chance, I would promise to try not to be gloomy. You said you would be at Haworth e're long, but that 'e're' has doubtlessly changed to 'ne'er', so I must wish to get to Halifax sometime to see you.

I saw Murray's monument praised in the papers and I trust you are getting on well with Beckwith's, as well as with your own personal statue of living flesh and blood.

Mine, like your Theseus, has lost its hands and feet, and I fear, its head also, for it can neither move write or think as it once could.

I hope I shall hear of you on John Brown's return from Halifax whither he has gone, and apologising honestly for putting you to the trouble of placing the enclosed in the hands of the newspaper Editor - if you choose to do so,

I remain, Dear Sir, Yours most sincerely, P.B. Brontë.

The 'enclosed scrap' was a poem entitled Penmaenmawr. It was heavily inspired by his feelings regarding Lydia Robinson, and would go on to be published in the Halifax Guardian.

28

TO JOHN FROBISHER - MARCH 1846

DEAR SIR,

I dare say you have forgotten both myself and a conversation in which, some years ago, I alluded to a favourite air – Glucks 'Mater divinae gratiae' as it is called in Novello's voluntaries, and 'Non vi turbate no' in Knights Musical Library.

I have ventured to compose English words on the recent stirring events in India adapted to the original air, and I do not know whether or not it would be worth your while to look over the manuscript and make what use you think best of it – or publish it as Glucks Air adapted to English words by myself – or arranged by Yourself – or under any title if it would deserve a title at all.

As I write in utter ignorance – and the stanzas were written to amuse an hour of long illness – excuse my intrusion upon your patience and believe me,

Your most respectful and ob't Servt,

P. Branwell Brontë

N.B. From the number of stanzas (eight) the air would have to be sung just twice over.

John Frobisher was the conductor of the Halifax Concerts and organist for the Halifax Parish Church.

29

TO JOSEPH BENTLEY LEYLAND - 28TH APRIL 1846

My Dear Sir,

As I am anxious - though my return for your kindness will be like giving a sixpence back for a sovereign lent - to do my best in my intended lines on "Morley" I want answers to the following questions;

Ist

- (As I cannot find it on the map or Gazzeteer) In what District of Lancashire is Morley situated?

IId

- Has the Hall a particular name?

IIId

- Do you know the family name of its owners when the occurrences happened which I ought to dwell on?

IVth

- Can you tell in what century they happened?

Vth

- What, told in the fewest words, was the nature of the leading occurrence?

If I learn these facts I'll do my best, but in all I try to write I desire to stick to probabilities and local characteristics.

Now, after troubling you so much, I doubt not that you will drive your fist through that damned medallion in your studio, as being the effigies of a regular bore.

I cannot, without a smile at myself, think of my stay for three days in Halifax on a business which need not have occupied three hours; but in truth when I fall back on myself I suffer so much wretchedness that I cannot withstand my temptation to get out of myself — and for that reason I am prosecuting enquiries about situations suitable to me whereby I could have a voyage abroad. The quietude of home, and the inability to make my family aware of the nature of most of my sufferings makes me write

"'Home thoughts are not, with me
Bright, as of yore;
Joys are forgot by me,
Taught to deplore!
My home has taken rest
In an afflicted breast
Which I have often pressed
But – may no more!"

Troubles never come alone — and I have some little troubles astride the shoulders of the big one.

Literary exertion would seem a resource, but the depression attendant on it, and the almost hopelessness of bursting through the barriers of literary ~~cliques~~ circles, and getting a hearing among publishers, make me disheartened and indifferent; for I cannot write what would be thrown, unread, in to a library fire: Otherwise I have the materials for a respectably sized volume, and if I were in London personally I might perhaps try Henry Moxon — a patronizer of the sons of rhyme; though I dare say the poor man often smarts for his liberality in publishing hideous trash.

As I know that, while here, I might send a manuscript to London, and say goodbye to it I feel it folly to feed the flames of a printers fire. So much for egotism!

I enclose a horrible ill drawn daub done to while away the times this morning. I meant it to represent a very rough figure in stone.

When all our cheerful hours seem gone forever; All lost that caused the body or the mind, To nourish love or friendship for our kind, And Charon's boat, prepared - oer Lethe's river - Our souls to waft, and all our thoughts to sever From what was once life's light, still there may be Some well loved bosom to whose pillow we Could heartily our utter self deliver: And, if - toward her grave - Death's dreamy road Our darling's feet should tread, each step by her Would draw our own steps to the same abode, And make a festival of sepulture; For, what gave joy, and joy to us had owed, Should Death affright us from, when he would her restore?

Yours most sincerely, P.B.Brontë.

A sketch is included in the letter. Titled 'Our Lady of Grief', the tablet beside the figure is engraved with 'NUESTA SENORA DE LA PENA'

The 'Morley' that Branwell alludes to is Morley Hall; at Bentley's behest, Branwell had embarked on an epic poetic history of the building.

30

TO FRANCIS GRUNDY - JUNE 1846

THE GENTLEMAN WITH WHOM I HAVE BEEN IS DEAD. HIS PROPERTY IS left in trust for the family, provided I do not see the widow; and if I do, it reverts to the executing trustees, with ruin to her. She is now distracted with sorrows and agonies; and the statement of her case, as given by her coachman, who has come to see me at Haworth, fills me with inexpressible grief. Her mind is distracted to the verge of insanity, and mine is so wearied that I wish I were in my grave.

Yours very sincerely,
P.B.BRONTË

The gentleman in question is Edmund Robinson, Branwell's erstwhile employer and husband to Lydia Robinson. Branwell would claim that Robinson's will stipulated that Lydia would be left penniless if she were to even see Branwell, but this isn't true.

This leaves us with the possibility that Branwell was lying, or that Lydia was lying to Branwell.

31

TO JOSEPH BENTLEY LEYLAND - JUNE 1846

Dear Sir,

I should have sent you "Morley Hall" ere now, but I am unable to finish it at present from agony to which the grave would be far preferable.

Mr Robinson of Thorp Green is dead, and he has left his widow in a dreadful state of health, she sent the Coachman to me yesterday, and the account which he gave of her sufferings was enough to burst my heart.

Through the will she is left quite powerless, and her eldest daughter who married independently, is cut off without a shilling.

The Executing Trustees detest me, and one declares that if he sees me he will shoot me.

These things I do not care about, but I do care for the life of the one who suffers even more than I do. Her Coachman said that it was a pity to see her, for she was only able to kneel in her bedroom in bitter tears and prayers. She has worn herself out in attendance on him, and his conduct during the few days before his death, was exceedingly mild and repentant, but that only distressed her doubly. Her conscience has helped to agonise her, and that misery I am saved from.

You, though not much older than myself, have known life. I now know it was a vengeance - for four nights I have not slept - for three days I have not tasted food - and when I think of the state of her I love best on earth, I could wish that my head was as cold and stupid as the ~~bust~~ medallion that lies in your studio.

I write very egotistically but it is because my mind is crowded with one set of thoughts, and I long for one sentence from a friend.

What I shall do I know not - I am too hard to die, and too wretched to live. My wretchedness is not about castles in the air, but about stern realities; my hardihood lies in bodily vigour; but, Dear Sir, my mind sees only a dreary future which I as little wish to enter on, as could a martyr to be bound to the stake.

I sincerely trust that you are well, and hope that this wretched scrawl will not make me appear to you a worthless fool, or a thorough bore.

Believe me, Yours, most sincerely, P B Brontë.

A sketch accompanies the letter, captioned only with 'Myself'.

32

TO JOSEPH BENTLEY LEYLAND - JUNE/JULY 1846

WELL, MY DEAR SIR, I HAVE GOT MY FINISHING STROKE AT LAST; AND I feel stunned into marble by the blow.

I have this morning received a long, kind and faithful letter from the medical gentleman who attended Mr B - in his last illness and who has since had an interview with me whom I can never forget.

He knows me well and he pities my case most sincerely, for he declares that though used to the rough ups and downs of this weary world, he shed tears from his heart when he saw the state of that lady and knew what I should feel.

When he mentioned my name she stared at him and fainted. When she recovered she in turns dwelt on her inextinguishable love for me — her horror at having been the first to delude me into wretchedness, and her agony at having been the cause of the death of her husband, who, in his last hours, bitterly repented of his treatment of her.

Her sensitive mind was totally wrecked. She wandered into talking of entering a Nunnery; and the Doctor fairly debars me from hope in the future.

It's hard work for me dear Sir; I would bear it - but my health is so bad that the body seems as if it could not bear the mental shock.

I never cared one bit about the property. I cared about herself - and always shall do.

May God bless her but I wish I had never known her!

My appetite is lost; my nights are dreadful, and having nothing to do makes me dwell on past scenes - on her own self, her voice, her person, her thoughts - till I could be glad if God would take me. In the next world I could not be worse than I am in this.

I am not a whiner dear sir, but when a young man like myself has fixed his soul on a being worthy of all love — and who for years, has given him all love, pardon him for boring a friend with a misery that has only one black end.

I fully expected a change of the will, and difficulties placed in my way by powerful and wealthy men, but I hardly expected the hopeless ruin of the mind that I loved even more than its body.

Excuse my egotism, and believe me, Dear Sir, Yours, P B Brontë

33

TO JOSEPH BENTLEY LEYLAND - 2ND JULY 1846

My Dear Sir,

John Brown told me that you had a basso relievo of my very wretched self, framed in your studio.

If it is a duplicate, I should like the carrier to bring it to Haworth; not that I care a fig for it, save from regard for its maker but my sisters ask me to try to obtain it; and I write the note in obedience to them.

I earnestly trust that you are heartier than I am and I promise to send you 'Morley Hall' as soon as dreary days and nights will give me leave to do so.

Believe me, yours most sincerely,P. B. Brontë.

34

TO JOSEPH BENTLEY LEYLAND - OCTOBER 1846

The letter is begun with a sketch comparing paradise with purgatory.

MY DEAR SIR,

Mr John Brown wishes me to tell you that if, by return of post, you can tell him the nature of his intended work, and the time it will probably occupy in execution either himself or his brother, or both will wait on you early next week.

He has only delayed answering your communication from his unavoidable absence in a pilgrimage from "Rochdale on the Rhine" to "the land of Ham" and from thence to Gehenna, Tophet, Golgotha, Erebus, the Styx and to the place he now occupies called Tartarus where he along with Sisyphus, Tantalus, Theseus, and Ixion lodge and board together.

However I hope that when he meets you he will join the company of Moses, Elias and the twelve prophets 'singing psalms sitting on a wet cloud' as an acquaintance of mine described the occupation of the blest.

"Morley Hall" is in the eighth month of her pregnancy and expects ere long to be delivered of a fine thumping boy whom its father means to christen Homer at the least, though the mother suggests that ' Poetaster ' would be more suitable; but that sounds too aristocratic.

Is the medallion cracked, that Thorwaldsen executed of AUGUSTUS CAESAR?

I wish I could see you; and, as Haworth's fair is held on Monday after the ensuing one, your presence then would gratify one of the fallen.

In my own register of transactions during my nights and days I find no matters worthy of extraction for your perusal: All is yet with me clouds and darkness, I hope you have, at least, blue sky and sunshine.

Constant and unavoidable depression of mind and body sadly shackle me in even trying to go on with any mental effort which might rescue me from the fate of a dry toast soaked six hours in a glass of cold water, and intended to be given to an old maid's squeamish cat.

Is there really such a thing as the "Risus Sardonicus' - the Sardonic laugh.? Did a man ever laugh the morning he was to be hanged?

35

TO JOSEPH BENTLEY LEYLAND - JANUARY 1847

DEAR SIR,

I had a letter written, and intended to have been forwarded to you a few days after I last left the ensnaring town of Halifax.

That letter, from being kept so long in my pocket book, has gone out of dates, so I have burnt it, and now send a short note as a precursor to an awfully lengthy one.

I have much to say to you with which you would probably be sadly bored, but as it will be only askings for advice I hope you will feel as a Cat does when her hair is stroked down. towards her tail. She purrs then; but she spits when it is stroked upwards.

I wish Mr Nicholson of the "Old Cock" would send me my bill of what I owe to him, and, the moment that I receive my outlaid cash, or any sum which may fall into my hands through the hands of one whom I may never see again, I shall settle it.

That settlement, I have some reason to hope, will be shortly.

But, can a few pounds make a fellow's soul like a calm bowl of creamed milk?

If it can I should like to drink that bowl dry.

I shall write more at length (Deo volente) on matters of much importance to me but of little to yourself.

Yours, in the bonds,
Sanctus
P B B
Patricius Branwellius Bronteio
Give my regards to Mr Frank.

36

TO JOSEPH BENTLEY LEYLAND - 24TH JANUARY 1847

My Dear Sir, I am going to write a scrawl, for the querulous egotism of which I must entreat your mercy, but, when I look upon my past, present and future, and then into my own self I find much, however unpleasant, that yearns for utterance.

This last week an honest and kindly friend has warned me that concealed hopes about one lady should ~~may~~ be given up let the effort to do so cost what it may. He is the Family medical attendant, and was commanded by Mr Evans M.p for North Derbyshire to return me, unopened, a letter which I addressed to Thorp Green and which the lady was not permitted to see. She too, surrounded by powerful persons who hate me like Hell, has sunk into religious melancholy, believes that her weight of sorrow is Gods punishment, and hopelessly resigns herself to her doom. God only knows what it does cost, and will, hereafter, cost me, to tear from my heart and remembrance the thousand recollections that rush upon me at the thought of four years gone by. Like ideas of sunlight to a man who has lost his sight they must be bright phantoms not to be realised again.

I had reason to hope that ere very long I should be the husband of a lady whom I loved best in the world and with whom, in more than competence, I might live at leisure to try to make myself an name in the world of posterity, without being pestered by the small but countless botherments, which like mosquitoes sting us in the world of work-day toil. That hope, and herself are gone; she to wither into patiently pining decline; I, to make room for drudgery falling on one now ill fitted to bear it.

That ill fittedness rises from causes which I should find myself able partially to overcome had I bodily strength, but with the want of that, and with the presence of daily lacerated nerves the task is not easy. I have been in truth too much petted through life, and in my last situation I was so much master, and gave myself so much up to enjoyment that now when the cloud of ill health and adversity has come upon me it will be a disheartening job to work myself up again through a new life's battle, from the position of five years ago to which I have been compelled to retreat with heavy loss and no gain. My army stands now where it did then, but mourning the slaughter of Youth, Health, Hope and both mental and physical elasticity.

The last two losses are indeed important to one who once built his hopes of rising in the world on the possession of them. Noble writings, works of art, music or poetry now instead of rousing my imagination, cause a whirlwind of blighting sorrow that sweeps over my mind with unspeakable dreariness, and if I sit down and try to write all ideas that used to come clothed in sunlight now press round me in funeral black; for really every pleasurable excitement that I used to know has changed to insipidity or pain.

I shall never be able to realise the too sanguine hopes of my friends, for at 28 I am a thoroughly old man - mentally and bodily - far more so indeed than I am willing to express. God knows I do not scribble like a poetaster when I quote Byron's terribly truthful words:

"No more, no more, oh! never more on me
The freshness of the heart shall fall like dew,
Which, out of all the lovely things we see
Extracts emotions beautiful and new!"

I used to think that if I could have for a week the free range of the

British Museum - the library included - I could feel as though I were placed for seven days in paradise, but now really, dear Sir, my eyes would roam over the Elgin marbles, the Egyptian saloon and the most treasured volumes like the eyes of a dead cod fish.

My rude rough acquaintances here ascribe my unhappiness solely to causes produced by my sometimes irregular life, because they have known no other pains than those resulting from excess or want of ready cash - they do not know that I would rather want a shirt than want a springy mind, and that my total want of happiness, were I to step into York Minster now, would be far, far worse than their want of a hundred pounds when they might happen to need it; and that if a dozen glasses or a bottle of wine drives off their cares, such cures only make me outwardly passable in company but never drive off mine.

I know, only that it is time for me to be something when I am nothing. That my father cannot have long to live, and that when he dies my evening, which is already twilight, will become night. That I shall then have a constitution still so strong that it will keep me years in torture and despair when I should every hour pray that I might die.

I know that I am avoiding, while I write, one greatest cause of my utter despair - but by God Sir it is nearly too bitter for me to allude to it!

For four years (including one year of absence) a Lady intensely loved me as I did her, and each sacrificed to that love all we had to sacrifice, and held out to each other HOPE for our guide to the future. She was all I could wish for in a woman, and vastly above me in rank, and she loved me even better than I did her - now what is the result of these four years? UTTER WRECK - the "Great Britain" is not so thoroughly stranded as I am. I have received today, since I began my scrawl, a note from her maid Miss Ann Marshall and I know from it that she has been terrified by vows which she was forced to swear to, on her husband's deathbed, (with every addition of terror which the ghastly dying eye could inflict upon a keenly sensitive and almost worried woman's mind) a complete severance from him in whom lay her whole hearts feelings. When that husband was scarce cold in his grave her relations, who controlled the whole property overwhelmed her with their tongues, and I am quite conscious that she has succumbed in terror, to what they have said.

To no one living have I said what I now say to you, and I should not bother yourself with my incoherent account did I not believe that you would be able to understand somewhat of what I meant - though not all Sir - for he who is without hope, and knows that his clock is at twelve at night, cannot communicate his feelings to one who finds his at twelve of noon.

I long to be able to see you, and I shall try to do so on Friday next - the 29th inst, or on Saturday - if I at all able to take the journey.

Till then I am, dear Sir, Yours Sincerely, P.B.Brontë

37

TO JOSEPH BENTLEY LEYLAND - JULY 1847

My Dear Sir,

I enclose the accompanying bill to tempt you to Haworth next Monday.

John Brown says he saw you lately, and that your looks spoke of hearty health.

For myself, after a fit of horror inexpressible, and violent palpitation of the heart, I have taken care of myself bodily, but to what good? The best health will not kill acute, and not ideal, mental agony.

Cheerful company does me good till some bitter truth blazes through my brain, and then the present of a bullet would be received with thanks.

I wish I could flee to writing as a refuge, but I cannot, and as to slumber, my mind, whether awake or asleep has been in incessant action for seven weeks.

Yours most truly, P.B. Brontë. Poor Dan Sugden has gone to the New Jerusalem. Alas, what is life?

38

TO JOSEPH BENTLEY LEYLAND - JANUARY 1848

DEAR SIR,

I send you, herewith, two scrawls on the beforehand page, which you had better burn the moment you see them.

I was really far enough from well when I saw you last week at Halifax, and if you should happen shortly to see Mrs Sugden of the Talbot you would greatly oblige me by telling her that I consider her conduct towards me as most kind and motherly, and that if I did anything, during temporary illness, to offend her I deeply regret it, and beg her to take my regret as my apology till I see her again; which, I trust will be erelong.

I was not intoxicated when I saw you last, Dear Sir, but I was so much broken down and embittered in heart that it did not need much extra stimulus to make me experience the fainting fit I had, after you left, at the Talbot, and another, more severe at Ms Crowthers in The Commercial Inn near the North gate.

When you return me the manuscript volume which I placed in your hands, will you (if you can easily lay your hands on it) enclose that MS called "Caroline" - left with you many months since - and which I should not care about any more than about the volume - only I have no copies of either.

When I feel a little better than I do at present I will write you a letter telling you more of my mind than I dare at present do, and leaving you to notice it or destroy it as you choose.

Wishing you all the happiness which the new year can bring, I am, Dear Sir, yours most truly, P.B. Brontë.

The letter includes these two sketches of "Patrick Reid" with a noose around his neck, and five figures around a table. The figures are named SUGDENIENSIS, DRACO THE FIREDRAKE, St John in the Wilderness, PHIDIAS, St Patrick alias Lord Peter.

39

TO JOSEPH BENTLEY LEYLAND - 22ND JUNE 1848

MY DEAR SIR,

Mr Nicholson has sent to my Father a demand for the settlement of my bill owed to him immediately, under penalty of a Court Summons.

I have written to inform him that I shall soon be able to pay him the balance left in full. For that I will write to Dr Crosby and request an advance through his hands which I am sure to obtain, when I will remit my amount owed, at once, to the Old Cock.

I have also given John Brown this morning Ten shillings which John will certainly place in Mr N's hands on Wednesday next.

If he refuses my offer and presses me with law I am RUINED. I have had five months of such utter sleeplessness violent cough and frightful agony of mind that jail would destroy me forever.

I earnestly beg you to see Nicholson and tell him that any receipt of money in asking, through Dr Crosby, is morally certain.

If you conveniently can see Mrs Sugden of the Talbot, and tell her that on receipt of the money I expect so shortly I will transmit her the whole or part of the account I owe her.

Excuse this scrawl - long have I resolved to write to you a letter of five or six pages, but intolerable mental wretchedness and corporeal weakness have utterly prevented me.

I shall bother you again if this painful business only gets settled.

At present believe me Dear Sir, yours, Sincerely but nearly worn out, P.B. Brontë.

40

TO JOSEPH BENTLEY LEYLAND
DATE? JUNE 1848?

FOR MERCIES SAKE COME AND SEE ME, FOR I HAVE SOUGHT FOR YOU TILL I dare not risk my knee and my eyesight any more this evening.

I shall have a bad evening and night if I do not see you but I hardly know where to send the bearer of this note, so as to enable him to catch you.

NORTHANGERLAND

41

TO JOHN BROWN - AUGUST 1848

SUNDAY.

Noon.

Dear John,

I shall feel very much obliged to you if can contrive to get me Five pence worth of Gin in a proper measure.

Should it be speedily got I could perhaps take it from you or Billy at the lane top or what would be quite as well sent out for, to you.

I anxiously ask the favour because I know the good it will do me.

Punctually at Half past Nine in the morning you will be paid the 5d out of a shilling given me then. Yours, P.B.B.

ACKNOWLEDGMENTS

When you write a book, you often do so in a room by yourself, but that doesn't mean you write it alone.

I am eternally indebted to my wife, who has put up with years of hearing "I should write a book about Branwell Brontë" before I finally sat down and did it.

This book would likely not exist without Ross Wilson, whose guidance and feedback was invaluable when I first wrote my dissertation on Branwell at the University of East Anglia.

Alison Neal was kind enough to send me a copy of an article that I just could not find anywhere else.

I did not forge this path myself. My travels through Branwell's world referred to maps left by others who went before. In this regard, Juliet Barker needs special mention for the stunning work she has done on all of the Brontës.

Finally, I'd like to thank you for reading this book. Whether you enjoyed it, hated it, or fell somewhere between, I hope it has made you take a fresh and favourable look at Branwell Brontë.

Printed in Great Britain
by Amazon

35784197R00178